Architecture and the Virtual

Architecture and the Virtual

by Marta Jecu

intellect Bristol, UK / Chicago, USA

Published in the UK in 2018 by
Intellect, The Mill, Parnall Road, Fishponds, Bristol, BS16 3JG, UK

Published in the USA in 2018 by
Intellect, The University of Chicago Press, 1427 E. 60th Street,
Chicago, IL 60637, USA

A catalogue record for this book is available from the
British Library.

Cover and layout design: Stephanie Sarlos
Copy-editor: MPS Technologies
Production manager: Heather Gibson

Print (paperback) ISBN: 978-1-78320-945-3
ePDF ISBN: 978-1-78320-257-7

Printed and bound by Short Run Press Ltd.

Acknowledgements

Warm thanks to all the artists and interview partners for their collaboration in the making of this volume, to my Ph.D. coordinators Renate Schlesier, Erika-Fischer Lichte and Christoph Wulf, to my present supervisor Jose Manuel Gomes Pinto, whose support made this publication possible, to Heather Gibson from Intellect Books for her patience and understanding, to my father Silviu Jecu, and to Fernando Veiras for his collaboration in the work with Hironari Kubota.

Contents

Fig. 0.1: Andrea Mantegna, St. Sebastian,
1480, Musée du Louvre, Paris, Detail
©Public Domain.

Fig. 0.2: Andrea Mantegna,
St. Sebastian, 1480, Musée du Louvre,
Paris, ©Public Domain.

Fig. 0.3: Carlos Bunga, Espacio Metaforico, 2010, Cardboard, paint and wood on Carrara marble pedestal, Sculpture at Postmonument: XIV Carrara International Biennale of Sculpture, Carrara, Italia, ©Carlos Bunga.

Fig. 0.4: Carlos Bunga, Espacio Metaforico, 2010, Cardboard, paint and wood on Carrara marble pedestal, Sculpture at Postmonument: XIV Carrara International Biennale of Sculpture, Carrara, Italia, ©Carlos Bunga.

Introduction

The multiple is not only what has many parts, but also what is folded in many ways.

(Deleuze 2006b: 3)

In late medieval painting, the preoccupation with ruins manifested itself by cloaking important religious scenes under the rugged abode of time-eaten ancient colonnades, cracked fronts and almost pulverized arches. Derelict and Roman remains, markers of another era in the history of devotion, are called to spatially situate 'The Nativity' or 'The Adoration of the Magi' in an eternal present. During the Renaissance, Greek and Roman ruined pieces advanced vigorously to carry entire constructional complexes that sturdily coffer hagiographic allegories in a complex composition of scenes, extracted from the quotidian, which were traced from antique friezes and methodically constructed. The ruin here is the architecture that carries information; it is a reservoir of erudition but most of all of an ancient tradition of urbanity. The well-felt cultural distance in time and space from ancient cosmopolitanism, which endows the ruin with symbolic authority and substance, serves as a theatrical setting, marking an elated reinforcement of the antique past in a Christian, humanist new vision. This structural function of the ruin in Renaissance painting also appears in Andrea Mantegna's 'St. Sebastian of the Louvre' (1480), where the saint is martyred directly against a passionately documented Roman column that is crowned by a heavy capital, his foot replicated by a marble Roman one – symbol of the triumph of Christianity over paganism. This scenographic insight into a narratively-chronicled hyperreality is juxtaposed on a background block of architecture which can be seen in Figure 0.1.

In Figure 0.1, the antique ruins seem to be an osmotic part of a tectonic sedimentation of various ages, with their architectural excrescences. This totally different treatment from the protagonist's ruin featuring the saint in the main scene; the calibrated measures and organicity devoid of allegorical assertion approximates this architectural detail to an almost modernist reading of form.

At this point, the detail comes close to another almost modernist disclosure of form, Carlos Bunga's 'Espacio Metaforico' (2010). In both cases the fragmentary volumes oscillate between the documentary and the fantastic. Their purity arises from an approach that does not engage architecture either as a setting, or as a referent for an underlying and exterior reality, but eliminates the symbolic and narrative substrata with which architecture can be approached. In the main scene in Andrea Mantegna's painting, the Roman ruin works as a mark of separation insulating two spiritual eras. The annihilation of one historic age is invested convincingly in the fortification of the other. Much more fragile, the architectural detail of the right corner of the painting is less dualistic, ignoring the architectural conventions of Christian iconography and its rendition of the dichotomy between transitory matter and eternal spirit. Similarly, Carlos Bunga's sculpture embodies a matter that is equally tellurian, elemental, abstract and essential. The construction reaches a point of indistinction between natural and artificial and, like in the painting, the border between formations of earth and artificially-built forms becomes indiscernible.

These two representations refer back to even older ways of depicting ruined architecture, by connecting it to its past, archetypal forms in time. This is exactly what defines ruins – they shift architecture into a past where it disintegrates into nature, and push nature into becoming a built form. In this sense, ruins not only measure time like a barometer, but also define, situate and perform an active role. Seemingly opposed to the apparent agency of the ruined column of St. Sebastian, it is actually in this detail that an active force of architecture manifests itself, while the past and future of form are shown as propagating and unfolding according to their own terms. Architecture here, and also in the work of Carlos Bunga, seems to represent an accumulation of time that carries other forms, objects and situations within itself. In this sense, both these representations bring with them an apparent sitelessness, which actually discloses the intensity of a virtual dimension with its own reality and agency that is fundamentally specific and responsive in time and space. The viewer stands not in front of an already fabricated symbolic epiphany, but integrated into the work; he is a constituent and real part of it.

The works and discussions gathered here centre around the virtual presence of architecture and the way it enacts with but also produces time. The architectural works of Carlos Bunga, Cristian Rusu, Hironari Kubota, Sancho Silva, Yukihiro Taguchi, and Sinta Werner are drawn together since they make a virtual side of architecture directly experienceable by working with tactile, minimal and conceptual means. At the core of this volume stands the hypothesis of embodying the virtual with analogue means and its possible uses and applicability in the quotidian environment in which these works intervene. The works discussed have simple and clear, almost modernist forms that bring about a return to archetypes of architecture and come very close to the idea of the model. Mostly ephemeral, they are non-symbolic, built around convertible or even empty space, and are non-narrative. At the same time, they elaborate an architecture that surpasses the limitations of the discipline itself and makes momentary interventions and alterations in the immediate urban environment in which it is placed. Social situations are converted and a historic material connected to the built form always comes to the surface.

For capturing the agency of these works, the concept of *catalytic space* is introduced, which delineates a specific approach to space practised in these and similar works. Taken from the field of chemistry, a catalyst is a substance that brings a process into being, through which a chemical reaction will be accelerated. The catalyst remains unconsumed in this process. The term is used here to designate a synthetic conception of built space and is connected to the operative presence of the constructions themselves that unfold an agency: exhibited or performed in a certain context, they determine a row of changes and catapult the configuration of space into structural mutation. Spaces with their specific cultural connotations and social experiences are altered – they are brought in transformation with the involvement of the audience – but in a fluctuating way. Perspectives are opened upon their different temporary cycles. Therefore the works make a virtual side of architecture tangible, in the sense of temporarily bringing otherwise un-manifested spatial potentialities of the specific situation in which the work intervenes into the actuality of the viewer.

The works manifest a post-digital thinking by incorporating the indistinctiveness between digital and analogue into organic materialities and sensory experiences. The interplay between digital, biological, cultural, and technological elements, between conceptual and real space, between embodied and virtual media are manifestedly post-digital. In this sense, the approach that these works practice makes a clear statement in the debates surrounding the post-digital experience. They demonstrate that the trajectory of digital thinking is continued through crossbreeding with analogue.

In the four chapters I follow up on conditions and means by which the virtual can be directly experienced in the conceptual space. The chapters introduce a plurality of approaches to *virtuality* as it relates to architecture, space and partially design. To argue for the value of an expanded definition of *virtuality* that is not limited to a ubiquitous approach to *digital* as merely computational and parametric, this volume stresses the role of tactile, material, physical and analogue processes in the materialization of the virtual – extracted from interviews and scrutiny in historic sources.

The interviews form the core of this volume. They are framed, on one hand, by an introduction that situates concerns expressed by the interview partners in a larger frame of theoretical and historic reference. On the other hand, they are associated with a collection of images of the artists' works referred to in the interviews. The interviews confer an intensive insight into the artists' manner of thinking and working, and into their approach to architecture. •

Introduction to the content

In *The Fold. Leibniz and the Baroque*, Deleuze (2006b) adopts and further develops Leibniz's term of 'the fold', a spatial paradigm that is, for him, a philosophical principle. Here Deleuze explains that a building is not one space and one site, but many spaces folded into many sites. This folding of space into other spaces is, for him, architecture: a multiplicity, where everything is always read and re-read but can never be assimilated in its entirety and which, as with any pleat, is a consequence of a movement.

The works invoked in this book show ways in which the accumulation of information layered in an environment, building or situation can be brought to the surface and put into circulation again. This 'moving'' of information has various consequences and uses in the quotidian, immediate reality in which these works intervene. It can be experienced ephemerally due to the agency that the works put into motion. The artists work with processes of destruction and reconstruction of representation, but also with transpositions of situations, objects and images from one media to another (for example from performance into video, from sculpture into performance). The works show how superimposed layers of information – the virtual presence of a built environment – can be used by the audience and urban passers-by.

On the line of thought initiated by Gilles Deleuze, the virtual is not understood as an illusion, or as an altered copy of reality, but as a fluctuating, temporary manifestation of the existing potentialities of a certain situation. As will be shown below, Deleuze has described the virtual as a *presence*, which, though situated in proximity to our material reality, has not been actualized. Following Henri Bergson, Deleuze regards the possible as the correlative of the real, since it will transform itself into reality and is no more than a past form of what later became real. In place of this relationship, Deleuze proposes the virtual and the actual; the virtual is real, but has no actuality in the present; the actual has no resemblance to the virtual – it neither limits it nor selects from it, as happens in the other equation.

In this sense the works presented in this volume temporarily actualize a world that is real, but has no actuality in the present – the world of potentialities of matter and of architecture. Making these perceivable determines a rethinking of the situation in which the works are inserted, with immediate cultural and social implications, which will be described in the interviews gathered here.

The virtual–actual relationship on which the works are based can be understood as their structuring layer. I connect the oscillation between these two states in the following chapters with different aspects, which are all drawn to explain how the experience of the virtual is possible with immediate, almost bricolage tools. Recent theories of post-conceptualism discuss the recuperation of the image, after its dissolution that the avant-garde aimed for and partially attained. As will be shown, the experience of the virtual here is connected on one hand to the consistent material presence that a post-conceptual approach brings. On the other hand, it is also connected to a new tendency, which is here interpreted as post–digital, that applies the thinking on the virtual of the digital age to minimal, almost modernist tools of representation. This material proximity that the works unfold in relation to a viewer is performative. Without superimposing video projections, sensors etc. on architecture, but rather by taking an analogue approach rooted in conceptualism and related to the early minimalism of the avant-garde, this approach to space is the result of an assimilation of the virtual experience, launched by the digital era with its juxtaposition and indistinctiveness between real and virtual.

It is also the interactions brought by the digital era that initiate the viewer in becoming a participant in this performative, enhanced reality, while being himself transformed and becoming part of the art object. The conception of the virtual, expressed by the artists in the following interviews, recalls again the vision of Gilles Deleuze of the virtual as a *dimension of experience*. Actualization of spatial potentialities takes place by involving the correlation between the recipient and the work in a determined social context. At the same time, through their performative agency, the works gain an independence from their creator, the artist, and take on an unpredictable course of development, which reflects the non-auctorial positioning of the authors towards towards their own works. The agency and the transformations of these installations in the social space will be illustrated in the interviews on pages 132–148.

Another idea that this volume proposes and that I approach in the second chapter is that the specific understanding of architecture that results from these works represents a late materialization of the philosophical architecture of Jacques Derrida, for which the discipline itself did not find a functional solution in the 1980s.

Introduction to the structure

This volume is structured in four chapters with their own theoretical background, which complement each other and the ideas expressed in the interviews. Issues like performativity, deconstructivism, conceptualism and theories of the virtual, which are mentioned in the analytical introduction and which build the four chapters, reflect the multiplicity of influences and materials that the artists are working with. The fully quoted discussions with the artists and the gallerists Noam Braslavsky, Daniel Lima and Michael Krome, conducted over a three-year time period, are less oriented towards presenting their work or professional history, but instead pursue perspectives of their creative and conceptual universe, while conferring the reader access into the thinking of these personalities. Instead of constructing a direct reinforcement of the theoreticians' texts with the artists' statements and works (or vice versa), this book stresses rather multiple points of conjunction between their ideas and those of other thinkers (artists or scholars) based on historic, theoretical or philosophical criteria. The discussions with the artists are regarded themselves as theoretical sources in the consideration of the virtual, therefore they are given an equal weight to the other sources in the economy of book. The chapters are a confrontation with the questions highlighted by the personal preoccupations of the artists; therefore, the theoretical input does not exhaust a specific theory, but rather points to associated contexts in literature and debate in order to suggest some directions in which these concerns can be further pursued. Small parts of interviews are also often quoted in the body of the text. They usually originate from interviews that are not included in the rest of the book and are meant to reinforce the argument.

The first chapter is dedicated to the comprehension of performativity as the quality of a work to manifest itself actively in a certain environment just by being there. The reading of performativity made by Dorothea von Hantelmann is invoked, which throws light on the way in which the environmental and immersible qualities of these constructions become *experienceable* for the audience and unfold their agency. I link interactivity, understood in the digital era as the capacity to access, participate and intervene in a foreign reality, to the possibility of producing the *new* in a certain concrete situation. As will be seen from the description of the works and from the interviews, the news that the works generate manifests itself in most of the situations through an event, which alters the quotidian course of action in an unexpected way.

In the second chapter I will get close to the notion of deconstructivism and sketch its essential role in contemporary thinking, starting with the postmodern current of the late 1980s. My intention is to propose the idea that recent conceptual works offer an accurate materialization of the architectural project of Derrida, formulated some decades ago. The deconstructive theory of Jacques Derrida, having been at that point transposed in a rather formal way into postmodern architecture, now finds a new form of existence in these performative and highly conceptual works of art. Although not making programmatic reference to Derrida's theory of a new architecture, these built forms meet Derrida's thinking and offer solutions to Derrida's philosophical proposals: they surpass the function of habitation, are transformative and essentially structured like an event – attributes that Derrida associated with the deconstructive 'architectural experience'.

In my attempt to identify means by which the experience of the virtual can take place, I draw in the third chapter on conceptualism and post-conceptualism. I consider the legacy of a certain direction in the neo-avant-gardes, a direction that placed high value on the material qualities of objects, especially relevant, partially by means of documentation. Based on the outcomes of the interviews, I will trace a connection between on one hand the minimal and conceptual art of the neo-avant-garde as tendencies of art's own dissolution into pure idea, which is related to the virtual (as something being there, but not in reality), and on the other hand documentation as a way to establish a relation to the context and its immediate material presence. Yves Klein, the German artists' group Zero, and the neo-avant-garde experiments of the Japanese Gutai group are all brought up as references by the artists during the discussion of their works. Similar to the works discussed here, the Gutai artists put processes of matter into motion without the narrative or symbolic content that still characterized other contemporary experiments of the neo-avant-garde.

The conceptual approach of the recent works discussed here, is often based on documentary practices, which have their roots in the neo-avant-garde's demolished representation. Documentation is a destructive intervention on the objects, their time and their image, which is inherited from even earlier, from what Walter Benjamin understands as the modern trauma of visuality.

In the fourth chapter the means by which the processes of the actualization of the virtual takes place become central. I will evoke notions like the ruin, the event and the simulacrum, that play a decisive role in a number of interviews. Carlos Bunga, for example, considers his works simulacra of architecture. Even his actions are for him simulacra of destruction and construction processes. Simulacrum, as a copy without a model, is therefore a means by which the new can be realized in reference to the real and has a specific regenerating power in the context in which it appears. It is a virtual real since virtuality (as it is understood by Gilles Deleuze) represents an approximation of the real that is not actual, and that deviates from reality. I follow Carlos Bunga's ideas and approximate the architectural environments that appear in this volume to simulacra, since they function as documents of what spaces could have been under other conditions. I will draw again on the role of documentation, which simultaneously records and produces reality in an event-like way therefore offering concrete solutions in specific social environments.

I will trace also a brief history of the young concept of post-digital, a term which I consider essential for the approach to the virtual which results from these works. Their ideas and solutions, as well as the interviews in this book fill the little theorized notion with a new content. They project a direction in which the thinking of the virtual catalysed by the digital could further unfold.

Introduction to the works

The works discussed here do not share the same formal vocabulary since they generate in different preoccupations with space and the built form, but they are all concerned with the agency and capacities of space. These mostly analogous constructed environments disclose a side of architecture that functions as an archive of time, and a sum of various past and future spatial configurations. Without constructing narrative subjects, or augmenting the real with illusory effects, they deal with the virtual through their concern with creating and making visible a multiplicity of potentialities of architectures and spaces that surpass a given time-space framework. Still, as will be shown, this virtual is not connected to the creation of an artificial environment of infinite possibilities, but instead emerges by involving everyday material from the social and cultural environment in which these site-specific works are situated, therefore formulating a polemic or political agency in their environment. The works come also close to design, creating new functions for the existing spaces, while giving concrete solutions for the optimizing of certain environments or by offering a new interpretation to spatial hierarchy.

This analogue approach to the virtual, connected to minimalism and the abstractions of conceptualism, mostly assumes very simple, manual forms of manifestation and traverses various media identities. The works can encompass at the same time architectural models and the spoken word, installation and staged discourse and drawing, animation and sculpture. By substituting video with a camera obscura, Sancho Silva, for example, scrutinizes what an analogue image is and techniques of observance connected to architectural form. He also uses basic building techniques to construct multifunctional wooden units that blur the distinction between sculpture and architecture, private and public space, but also actual and virtual living space.

The works are not especially innovative from a formal perspective; they cite paradigmatic architectural forms but understand architecture as transcending its physical borders. As Boris Groys demonstrates, in his book 'Art Power' (2008), there is no difference between new and old at the level of visuality, in the sense that it is not possible to create a total difference in relation to what has been before. Groys explains that contemporary artwork operates with the 'different' rather than with the 'new', and places more emphasis on the context than on an absolute formal innovation.

Carlos Bunga often mentions that he does not conceive of his own working process with space as an auctorial performance (in the sense of space being a container for his own innovative acts and for creating a new artistic product), but as a way of making visible for an audience the intrinsic potentialities that space itself carries. His idea has been an inspiration for this book. His works, whose meaning cannot be located in a final product, are built by him of fragile materials, such as cardboard and tape, in a complex, time-consuming and manual process. He sometimes destroys his space-filling installations, even before the opening of an exhibition. Construction and destruction, with which he approaches sculpture and drawing, provoke modifications of the qualities of objects, accelerate or slow down time and map an initial object *in absentia*. He projects space by negating it, while he exposes gaps in signification, architectonic remains, which belong to a time of the 'after'.

'*Um-Räumen*', re-spacing space, is what Yukihiro Taguchi is doing with space. As with the other artists, he is redefining the composition of space in various media. He brings architecture into movement by decomposing it progressively and letting its parts travel in space. Then he reconstructs them in videos that use the stop-motion technique and reveal a space of their own. Without bringing anything new into space and without taking any existing element out of space, he is focusing on the relationships that emerge between its different elements, and which determine self-generating processes that construct his work in time. Taguchi lets the space shift from one situation into another, until different possibilities of its inner relationships manifest themselves concretely. His row of works 'Moments' deconstructs existing buildings and lets their elements wander around the city, by constructing other functional installations with them at every new station. This *operative* space in his interventions is always connected with human presence, seen in a social or a very intimate hypostasis. Spaces appear through our relationship with them, through the movements of the city, and his installations begin to function in a very concrete way through these interrelated forces.

Sancho Silva is working with the dismantling of pre-connoted constructed space, involving, in particular, vision and its cultural determinants. His works are tautological up to the point that they become non-existent. His installations may consist of various entrances to the work, of hidden mechanisms, which sustain and at the same time destroy the constructed space, and of machines or cabins, which simultaneously direct vision upon the city and upon the mechanisms themselves. His analogue, minimal and architectonic spaces are performative, in the sense that they call into presence political, historical and social systems of reference in distorted reflections. His works seem to become *indispensable* for the constitution of meaning of these culturally charged reference frames. In a subtle interplay of authority between subject and subjected, his constructed space disappears in spatial and temporal conjunctions, which Silva dismantles and de-conspires.

The work of Hironari Kubota is a mixture of elements of ancestral beliefs from Japanese culture and industrial and postindustrial elements, and it brings to life rituals and acts that are re-signified by the artist according to his own contemporary spirituality. Kubota creates architectures of various gyrating objects at high velocity until he completely destroys their initial identity, delimiting a recovered space that releases a virgin symbolic capital. He spins cars, boats and idols or bringing into movement huge handmade industrial machines – mammoths from another era – while imprints of animist worship get superposed with the traces of our own consumed civilization. He literally breaks the iconographic context of the image and frees the object from its temporal determination. In the spinning performances the objects seem to lose their self, as they leave behind their shape, their contours, their materiality. Almost flying, these initially inert, dense and massive objects are completely dissipated while not only their functionality but their representation itself is momentarily abolished. During the spinning process, Kubota uses popular music from Japan, which is played back by him with a modified rhythm and pitch, in a slight counter-movement with the rotations of his spinning objects. His shows determine the return of the individual to himself and formulate a symbolic rejuvenation of the object, a post-object in an altered time-space framework, which releases a certain tension. This oscillation of the mutated objects transgresses the given reality and reaches into an impossible condition, one that affirms a new and freed object that is beyond visual conventions. While working with the forces that are latent in the elements, he uses minimal techniques and addresses the problem of the fundamental devices of 'form giving'. The heavy sculptures begin to move in an elementary manner, but with a temporality that seems to belong to foreign cycles. Hironari Kubota constructs his artworks during many months of continuous work. Nevertheless his performances only last about 30 minutes, during which elements of urban pop culture mix with ritualistic religious moments and a contemporary architectural and sculptural vision. His works are intensive and do not take into account conventional frameworks of significance, surpassing genres yet expressing a futuristic and at the same time archaeological vision of materiality, movement and spatial definition.

Sinta Werner explores the domain of the optical illusion in sculptural installations that reproduce reality, feigning its apparent continuity, imponderability and fluidity with concrete, persistent materiality. She works with a space that is built with the instruments of the real, but differs imperceptibly from it. In her works, illusion is a provocative medium of reality analysis that moves beyond the mirror-effect and becomes a reflexion on the collision between reality and surreality.

Cristian Rusu starts working with space through what he calls *spatial clichés*. These are not so much stereotypes as they are cultural imprints on forms of representation and perception, which transport an implicit, historically-shaped, ideological load. His search is directed towards utopia – mental constructions, which are impossible to create materially, yet which function with persuasive power and come near to the aesthetic category of the sublime. Among other media, Cristian Rusu, like Carlos Bunga, works with architectural models, which question the laws of spatial representation. He represents architecture by oscillation of the basic form, which is connected to the multiplication and migration of architectural forms in time and with the cultural memory they convey. This subtle imbalance creates a disjunction between space and time and the specific rhythms thereof. It raises the question of instability of value, and makes a subtle subversive manoeuvre that abstracts the processes through which cultural identity is stated in architecture.

The way these spaces lead the narrative content of a given situation and of concrete experiences into abstraction brings a register of intensity and is a meditation on destruction and decay over time. The works keep the clarity of elementary forms, but like ruins, they carry a thick history of material presence and a history of cultural form. They embody paradigmatic architectural elements, which resonate with the fluctuating limits of the discipline itself, which revisit the same shapes every time with new content: essential architectural moulds, which now cannot be considered beyond the heavy sedimentation of connotations acquired thus far. •

CHAPTER 1
Intensity: Performativity and the virtual

I am for my work, what is called in traditional Japanese theatre, a kuroko: a character, all dressed in black (his face is covered too), who assists the theater from the backstage, who prepares the stage, who gives directions to the actors and sometimes appears on the stage, but always remains unnoticed. Without his presence in the background the theatre could not move forward. Still he has to always stay hidden, even though he appears in the foreground. This is the best position that I could take for my work. If I mingle too much with my work, then I will make a work about my-self, but I would like to keep the work, as work, always in the foreground. My work exists only with the presence of the audience, without them my work would not be possible. I wish for the audience to act inside my work, without me taking an authoritarian role in this process. The audience and myself, we can be both actors in this play. To do this, one of my strategies is to upload my films and the documentation of my work onto YouTube. Everyone can re-use my works, appropriate them, as with any other material.

(Taguchi 2008)

Besides being site-specific and reacting to a specific cultural or political context, the works reproduced in this volume subsume simultaneously a multiplicity of possibilities that an initial situation can carry and surpass the limits of the present by addressing various temporal layers. Performativity is a key concept that is mentioned frequently during the discussions quoted here. It is a means of explaining how a mostly analogue, minimally built environment can transmit a virtual dimension, capable of being experienced, that expands the space beyond its sphere of visibility in the present. Performativity establishes a connection between the work and its environment, and embodies the effects upon its surroundings that it influences and shapes. These performative architectures are therefore temporary, fluctuating and subject to change. In considering these works, and in the talks with the artists about their approach to architecture and site-specificity, the *reality that a work generates* stays at the core of these discussions. It will be shown in the following pages in which way performativity is seen as the agency by which the virtual can temporarily actualize and how this is thought of, in conjunction with an already assimilated digital experience.

In 'Moment' (2008), Yukihiro Taguchi's first piece from 'Moments', a series of works that he calls 'performative', he lifted up the wooden floor panels of the gallery and constructed with them every day another installation inside the gallery. One hundred additional drawings showed possibilities of arrangements for the wooden bars. The gallery changed into a landscape of slopes, which seemed a cityscape, an archaeological site or a street in construction, while the panel installations could be used for table tennis, a cinema, a party setting or a large dinner table, on which Taguchi himself served sushi. In 'Moment. Performatives Spazieren' (2008) he decided to take the wood panels outside of the gallery into public space, and mingled them with various objects or constructions found on the streets of Berlin Kreuzberg. Every day he constructed new functional installations with them, which were usable and became urban furniture that generated their own social practices.

Brief historic overview of the term

The term 'performativity' comes from John Austin in his 1955 lecture 'How to do Things with Words' (Austin 1962) where he defines a 'performative utterance' as one that should not be considered true or false from the point of view of its content, but from the point of view of the factual realization of the action, which it describes verbally. In this case speaking is doing. The performative utterance brings an action into being, solely through its expression. Although Austin is excluding art in his consideration, his theory had a decisive role in art theory and slightly preceded the movement of the avant-gardes. Austin excludes all the arts, and, with reference to the theatrical field, suggests: 'a performative utterance will, for example, be *in a peculiar way* hollow or void if said by an actor on the stage, or if introduced in a poem, or spoken in soliloquy'. (Austin 1962: 22). Theatrical/artistic utterances are not included by him in the performative utterances he envisions, since they do not represent 'normal' speech. Therefore theatrical utterances cannot realize that which they express: 'Language in such circumstances is in special ways – intelligibly – used not seriously, but in ways *parasitic* upon its normal use' (Austin 1962: 22). Nevertheless, Austin's theory has determined the emergence of the 'performative turn' in various cultural arenas. Transferred into the domain of the visual arts it brought the understanding that alone through the existence of a work, through its self-assertion, its expressive potential manifests and can influence its environment.

Recent approaches that regard theoretical argumentation from the point of view of its dramatic and aesthetic value also have as a starting point the performativity of any type of utterance. Austin's book is considered as having made a step in this direction, by not only exposing a theory, but by also performing it: the rhetoric of his argumentation has been seen as

Fig. 1.1-3: Yukihiro Taguchi, Moment, 2008, Galerie Air Garten, Berlin, ©Yukihiro Taguchi.

a performative demonstration itself. Shoshana Felman (1983), for example, is not considering the 'what' in Austin's work, but mostly the 'how'. Felman's reading of Austin reveals what she calls Austin's Don Juanisms: his humour and his sense of spectacular demonstration, although his theory is not worked out systematically and has argumentative gaps. This theatrical ambiguity of Austin is, for Felman, a demonstration of the performativity of his theory itself, which emerges particularly from the failure of his theory: 'The very performance of the performative consists precisely in performing the loss of footing. It is the performance of the loss of ground' (Felman 1983: 151).

In its 'failure', the applicability of Austin's theory is evident. As opposed to a decree, performativity is an utterance that tolerates the possibility of its negation and makes place for ambiguity, as does the argumentation of Austin too. The performativity of an artwork has the power to set into being that which it represents. Even though it does not represent the formulation of a definitive statement, and is itself subject to oscillation and fluctuations, a work of art can, nevertheless, set the frame of a possible dialogue, but only in the likelihood of an open and permeable structure.

Jacques Derrida's deconstructive reading of Austin shifts the focus of the analysis from the utterance as an individual expression to societal conventions and subordinates. In his analysis he transfers the individual relevance to a social one. His attention goes beyond the individual, intentional act to the infinite repetitions and processes, in which difference and similarity condition and at the same time enable, in a broader social field, a free and innovative agency of the individual. Derrida argues that no performative utterance could be successful if it does not represent a quotation in order to be recognizable (Derrida 1988a: 310).[1]

Through repetition and a new reading in a certain context, which is itself never absolutely determinable and saturated, a difference appears. Meaning is therefore always relational, never absolute, and difference is a counterpoint to identity. In Derrida's vision, the potential of a work is being read as a cultural statement, which is formed by the different contexts of its reception. The work is a result of the layering of meaning by its various recipients.

Mieke Bal (2009: 1–15) also talks about the relationship between performativity and performance in light of the individual – social connection. In a brief article (2009: 91–106) she differentiates between the terms 'performance' and 'performativity' as follows: 'Performance, the unique realization of a work, belongs to another order than performativity, an aspect of a work that does what it says' (Bal 2009: 93). Mieke Bal understands performativity along the lines of Austin, as the emergence of an action in the here and now. Bal connects performativity with a *charm*, which belongs to the present, and is released by the presence of objects or situations in the moment of their occurrence. At the same time, Bal stresses, besides this charm, the embedding of performance in culture.[2]

Bal talks about the 'here and now' of performativity, which functions similarly to the occurrence of an event. The intensity with which the performative character of a work emerges is therefore connected to its immediacy, which can be regarded as a momentary actualization of potentialities that a situation carries.

It was Judith Butler who started to extend the approach of performativity to cultural domains like the social sciences, by stressing, in her book *Bodies That Matter,* that the reduction of performativity to performance would be a mistake (Butler 1993: 234). Also, for Dorothea von Hantelmann, a demarcation between the areas of significance of the two concepts *performance* and *performativity* is essential in the field of contemporary art. Performativity is regarded by Dorothea von Hantelmann (2007) as being a quality of works of art to manifest themselves, to articulate in an expressive way, to become explicit and to gain in this way a power to create reality. This power develops independently from the work's content.

> The performativity of a work of art is the *reality* which it manifests by the force of its existence at a place, in a situation, by the force of its production, reception and lasting. Performative is an allegation, the power to create reality […]. The performative dimension designates the bounding of art in a reality, which every single work is also generating.
>
> (Hantelmann 2007: 12)

As an interpretative paradigm and as an analytical model, performativity could be applied, in principle, to any work of art. Each work is performative merely due to its presence and can therefore be assimilated solely by how it affects the viewer and how it acts. From this line of thought, the relationship between the work and its spatial and discursive context is immediately deducible. Performativity makes concrete a potential for action, which is based in the conjunction of art with the domain of the social. Through the performative dimension of a work, its relevance becomes 'not the work as signifier, but its factual existence that represents the initial point of an artistic potential for action and affirmation' (Hantelmann 2007: 18).

Consequences of performativity: Non-auctoriality, questions of media, polemic intervention

In the interviews that I conducted with the artists, very often the differentiation between performativity and performance plays a crucial role with regard to a nuanced understanding of their work. The artists discuss their work not as a singular, unrepeatable auctorial gesture, but comment rather on the intrinsic statement that a built space carries: by its existence in a certain place; by belonging to a certain cultural climate; by its use that is conferred by various social actors. This definition of the work is based on the rejection of the model of the artist as creator of a subjective universe, which is symbolically coded according to a narrative content constructed by him or her. On the contrary, the work is seen as an ongoing performative project that has an autonomous presence, can change in time, and is subject to correlations. In this sense, the non-auctorial work can be understood as a sedimented presence in which historic layers of cultural significance have been deposited, while their performative presence triggers processes that expand their physical conditions.

Yukihiro Taguchi generally refers to his work as performative because 'it is the space that realizes the

Fig. 1.4-5: Yukihiro Taguchi, Visitor, 2007, Sarajevo, ©Yukihiro Taguchi.

performance, it is not a performance by me or the audience' (Taguchi 2008). In the work of Taguchi it is the speculative use of media that brings social issues up. In most of his works he makes use of the 'stop-motion technique' and constructs a dynamic and fictionalized movement-documentation of his installations. The performativity of the situation depicted emerges by joining still images of his actions into an animated video. Taguchi brings movement into matter that is directly experienced through the mediation of film and its intervention in the temporality of the depicted events. In his video 'Visitor', made in 2007 in Sarajevo, spatial performativity becomes a force that can shape human relations, but also embody the power that the public space exercises over the individual. Without staging a dramatic happening in public space, Taguchi merely medially frames its presence by photographing himself with various passers-by in front of a public monument for the victims of the Second World War. The work shows how the translation from one media to another (action to photography to video) can produce an awareness of the political charge of space that results from a constant re-positioning and mental re-presentation (on both a public and a personal level) of cultural capital in space.

I have spent many days in the surroundings of this monument and have observed the specific temporal rhythm of this place. The space that resulted around this symbolic flame interested me, in the sense that it has developed its own performance. The tourists that spent time on the same spot had shaped a situation, an event, a meaning, by spending a fragment of their own time in this place. The consecutive moments of each of them were separated in time, just as they were separate in space, but the monument consists of these superimposed spatial fragments. In my film I have just joined together all these moments into one and the same spatial frame (using the stop-motion technique), and have constructed, therefore, a new continuity. Through this I wanted to direct the perspective from the people to the space. The space becomes the actor and the actions of the people become the actions of the space. Photography is a very suitable medium for doing that: I have joined separate images (since all these moments are separately experienced by each of these people recorded) into a video, in order to show that, for me, what is of ultimate importance is the performance of the space itself. The presence of all the tourists in different timeframes, in the same place, creates a layering, which I regard as an autonomous spatial reality, and which is depicted in this video.

(Taguchi 2008, personal communication)

In some of the actions that Taguchi performs in space, danger, and the experience of various tensions that inhabit space, is another means by which the spatial potential can be experienced. In his installations 'Surface' (2003), 'Spannung' (2003) and 'Supportable Space' (2003), Taguchi tests the forces of space. These vectors of tension that support space are made visible through the instability of space, as another signifier that can draw attention to and even make visible the powers of space: the wooden sticks, for example, can collapse on the viewer with any micro-modification of their position. Space is shown by Taguchi as an inherently dynamic structure. In his work 'Domino' (2006), the private library of a gallerist, arranged like a set of dominoes, is brought into motion by the minimal gesture of turning over a single book. The book-space, as an interior space of experience, is a space of information opened performatively in a 'readable form'.

The work of Sancho Silva brings to the awareness of the viewer spatial forms of organization. He transposes functions of some architectonic elements unto others: a roof is functionally different from a window, but in his work their functional logic shifts. These modifications generate differing temporal sequences, as each architectonical element brings with it another temporality (in watching architecture, in traversing architecture, in staying in architecture). In Silva's work these different moments get almost confounded and this creates an estrangement effect. In the work 'Shortcut' (2002) Sancho Silva has constructed a passage from one street to the next street *through* a house. He calls this shortcut a distortion, something that has been twisted:

> I propose an enigma, and the public is invited to solve the puzzle. This mental process is embodied in the movement of the person who is experiencing it. The work is to be used, it is not only visual, and I base my work on this duality as a dialectical experience.
>
> (Silva 2007 interview)

Shortcuts permit the emergence of a new spatial configuration that reveals performatively a possible order underneath, which directs, controls and deceives the viewer, but also extends/ augments his physical capacities. This extension of the human with *devices* that are artificial, yet always constructed through the most basic means, is shown as being at hand and ubiquitous in our social environment. This human perception, framed by architectural devices that develop their own economy of influence, is always politically charged in Silva's work, with obvious connections to the *panopticon type* of institutional building.

Here is a fragment of an interview regarding his use of spatial devices. This interview was conducted at the Pinksummer Gallery in Genoa, Italy, which represents Sancho Silva's work (Silva 2003):

Fig. 1.6: Yukihiro Taguchi, Supportable Space, 2003, Tokyo, ©Yukihiro Taguchi.

Fig. 1.7: Yukihiro Taguchi, Domino, 2006, Rotterdam, ©Yukihiro Taguchi.

S.S.:   V*ision* is one way to create space. Space, in general, structures perception, like a house, for example, which structures your vision through doors and windows from the inside to the outside. Vision is also an important element in the construction of space. This is not the only one, because there is also *movement*. I use movement by giving different possibilities of movement to the person who inhabits a space: using corridors, different routes to go from point A to point B, or blocking different passages and opening others. Architecture determines movement, determines how you do different movements. In and of itself it gives instructions; it directs.

P: Where does this lead you then?

S.S.:   I am interested in abstracting the potential of the space in terms of architecture. Usually you live in these environments and you are not aware so much how it affects you, how it shapes what you see, how you move. I try to create a force which stabilizes this potential. That is why I do constructions that deny the function of space, so you become aware of these mechanisms of manipulation. I always try to have two points of view in the works: one point of view in which you are immersed in a mechanism and you cannot orient yourself in it and you cannot understand it – you are controlled by it. Then I try to construct a second point of view within the same work, to see it from outside, to see how it works. You can then dismantle the mechanism in your mind. […]

P: In some ways your work refers to the analytic cubism of Picasso and Braque. In 'Overviewer' (a project presented in 2001 at the Serralves Museum in Porto) the viewer could look under the wall in front of the windows of the museum through a periscope. Does this kind of passing beyond the physical perception with a periscope refer to knowledge and again to time – time of memory – in which we can know even what we cannot see?

S.S.:   In 'Overviewer' I attached a periscope to the right half of a window that would otherwise look directly onto a wall. The left side of the window was left uncovered. When looking through the window you could see the wall on the left and on the right, a tunnel that appeared to go through the wall and reveal its other side. The result was, on the one hand, an alteration of the topological structure of visual space: two places that were previously visually disjointed were now visually connected. On the other hand, and because of this topological shift, the visual components of the space were themselves severed from the architectural and ergonomic ones. Maybe there is a parallel with analytic cubism, but in my work the spatial components are not separated in time. They are inherently separate.

P: You wrote that the central concept of your work is space. The idea of space is not univocal, but takes different shapes and meanings in different fields: from mathematics to philosophy, from economic sciences to the social, while urban designs conceive of space in their own way, apparently autonomously. You said that discovering the connection established by history, by the time between the different concepts of space is an endless work, but definitely significant. Is this what you pursue with your work?

Fig. 1.8: Carlos Bunga, Mausoleum, 2012, Site specific installation, Pinacoteca do Estado de São Paulo, São Paulo, ©Carlos Bunga.

S.S.:   Not exactly. I don't think my work develops according to a precisely determined philosophical project. It is not guided by strict methodological principles. I think it operates according to its own logic and, conceptually speaking, its movements are quite unpredictable. What happens is that once I look back at my works I try to articulate them according to a conceptual scheme. Slowly this conceptual scheme gains its own momentum and begins to take a specific direction that is not necessarily parallel to that of the works. What this means is that there is always a tension between the works and the conceptual scheme that envelops them. Surely, the conceptual scheme will punctually influence the trajectory of the works, but it does not guide it. That being said, I can say that I have a big interest in the history of space, how its furthermost limits and its overall shape have changed, how it has been treated

Fig. 1.9-1.10: Carlos Bunga, Annotated newspaper material, ©Carlos Bunga.

philosophically and scientifically, how it has been articulated, categorized, constructed and represented across history. I think this will help us understand what space is today, and to what extent it acts and forms the world.

A constant critical dimension is prevalent not only in the work of Sancho Silva, but in the approaches of the other artists as well: every space is the result of a cultural policy. The works show situations as evolving on their own, while their ideological connotations become obvious.

Bunga started his work, on the one hand through the approach of interiority in architecture and on the other hand as a discourse on transformation of institutional architecture, by building over museum spaces, galleries and banks until they were unrecognizable. This moment of transformation is not a technical mutation, but rather what Bunga calls a *pictorial* space. In his ambiguous constructions he works also with what could be called 'documentary alterations', which modify past forms of his present constructions. Bunga also collects media images and old photographs that document destroyed buildings or transformed urban landscapes that resulted from a natural disaster, war or radical urban change. For him they represent moments of inversion of temporal cycles, when an accident can accelerate the temporality of a building or an urban configuration.

In an interview, Bunga (2010 interview) describes the fact that there is a connection for him between the processuality[3] of a construction-deconstruction process and the action of documenting. For him, documentation does not only archive events, but also their potentialities; it records a situation according to what it *could* have been. It is therefore documentation that makes a performative approach to space possible in his work. Not working with any type of digital manipulation in deviating the course of his previously built environments, but solely in a constructional, analogue way, Bunga attains the realization of this virtual spatiality,[4] by using the inherent qualities of representation.

In his space-filling installations new spaces appear as *spatial intervals* between, outside, under or superimposed on other buildings, and these are painted in monochromatic colour fields. Bunga is often building and then destroying his own constructions in performances, or destroying them even before the opening. What is visibly left over are only fine marks of something that remains unrevealed to the exhibition visitor. Departing from circumstantial evidence, he recreates not the reality that had taken place in that space, but one that might have been. In some of his works he displays only emptiness that which resulted from his complete destruction of previously built installations. His work ranges from huge installations, such as 'Metamorphosis' at the Miami Art Museum (2009/2010), to tabloid displays, such as the 'The Phaidon Atlas of Contemporary World Architecture' (2008), in which the reference book has gone through a paper shredder and is displayed as a landscape of *remains*, or to an architectonical sculpture, like his works in the 14th Biennial of Carrara (2010) or his works in Zona Maco Sur, Mexico (2010). His drawings, or sculptural objects of indistinct forms, propose a moment of 'the after', after a shift, without revealing where and when.

In his project 'Marxitecture', shown in 2009 in Gallery Krome, Berlin, the critical note becomes obvious. Bunga simply layered/collaged various politically charged architectural prototypes into one single framework: the Marxist architectural environment of Karl-Marx-Allee in the former Eastern part of Berlin; the contemporary gallery itself located in a paradigmatic building from that historical period; and Bunga's own temporary cardboard construction. The commentary that emerges is directed towards the deficient functional principles of urbanism and gaps due to forced urbanistic measures in the Soviet architecture imposed in the former German Democratic Republic (DDR). These architectural malfunctionings, mentioned by Michael Krome in the interview on pages 63-66 (Krome 2009), are still felt by the citizen in the daily experience, but are built over by other structures. Bunga's cardboards allow the eye to freely adopt multiple perspectives on the distanced, vacuum-sealed representational architecture of Karl-Marx-Allee, particularly in its emphasis on the ceremonial exterior.

Fig 1.11: Carlos Bunga, Marxitecture, 2009, Exhibition view, Galerie Krome, Berlin, ©Carlos Bunga, Galerie Krome.

> ''Marxitecture' relates principles of modular architecture and pre-fabrication, both of which display an extensive use of the grid in the tradition of the Bauhaus as well as in Socialist mass housing (the typical Berliner *Plattenbau*/concrete apartment buildings), transforming Bunga's installation into an associative, fragmentary image. […] 'Marxitecture' can be seen as a continuation of the diverse processes of transition present in Bunga's work.[5]

(Krome 2009)

Performativity as emerging from the contemporary structure of representation

In a dense article dedicated to performativity, Delfim Sardo (2007) describes it from a cultural–analytical point of view, as the 'space between two images'. This is for him the paradigmatic space of the culture of the gaze and of perception, which has emerged from the structure of representation in the 20th century. Distinct images were connected to each other according to a concept – either through cinema, through a form of exhibition, or by a curator or by cultural analysis (for example the one established by Aby Warburg). This connection determined that the new emergent succession of images lacked a temporal natural continuity in their structure of representation. It also created a culture governed by a relational aspect and introduced the presence of the audience as a constitutive element of the work. The audience functioned from now on as the binding agent of the work. Delfim Sardo shows, therefore, that the art of the 20th century set as its goal the creation of connections and relations. Performativity is exercised, according to Sardo, in the mobile definition of a net of expectations (Sardo 2007: 413). For Sardo, the mystery that we attribute to art also originates in this field between two images. Referring to the term 'interval', with which Aby Warburg denominated his own method of iconology, Sardo calls performativity the gap between two images. The movement that the spectator has to perform is always a jump, which is indispensable for the new relational work. Sardo calls Warburg's method a jump in-between different cultural domains, which deconstructed every form of succession or evolution of styles. Warburg's way of approaching cultural information places importance on experience, and on the oscillation between different possible connections (Sardo 2007: 413). This is, in essence, a cinematographic method of montage that offers to the receiver of the work, the possibility to assimilate elements and to build his own path in the process of absorption of the work, where every work functions like a prototype for a future image (Sardo 2007: 415). Sardo considers space as the object of the work itself, as was conceived for example by Kurt Schwitters' 'Merzbau' or Yves Klein's 'Vide', where the interval became immanent to the work. The spectator was then invited to step inside this space, to occupy and experience it. The works themselves remained unfinished since the spectator became the carrier of the meaning of the work, and because experience remains unpredictable.

The movement of the spectator is not substitutive, but concrete inside the three-dimensional work. Therefore agency and performance, not representation, stand at the core of this work, and the audience becomes the force of the existence of the work. Performativity, concludes Sardo, belongs to the work and can be transferable to the space. Performativity legitimizes the possibility of the existence of a mobile, placeless art, which emerges through contact with its recipients. This place of art is one that has no fixed parameters for Delfim Sardo, but which can be tested in every moment through the connections that it creates (Sardo 2007: 413).

Performativity and the virtual

Having in mind these definitions of performativity, its role in the experience of the virtual comes now into focus. A very particular understanding of performativity results from Gernot Böhme's vision on virtual space. We can extract the qualities of a performative space from his definition of the 'space of physical presence', which is at the same time for him 'a space of action and atmosphere'. Böhme (2004: 129–140) is following his constant preoccupation with atmosphere, when he poses the question 'What is space?'. In this context, his investigation of space and his terminological differentiations can deliver the fundamental means with which virtual space can be delimited for further analysis. He is scrutinizing space firstly regarding the essence of our denomination of space, and secondly, connected to that, regarding the nature of virtual spaces. Böhme also questions the possibility of the differentiation of the multiplicity of modes of conception and experiences of space, and asks if we can talk about an essence of space, which could correspond to and reunite all spatial categories. The main distinction regarding types of space, for Gernot Böhme, is that between the medial space as a space of representation and the experiential space as the space of our physical presence. In his analysis he takes as a starting point an initial superposition of the two concepts of Immanuel Kant (1998: 4–15) and reads Kant's interpretation in the sense of a demarcation between inner and exterior perceptions of space. The inner perception is that of the subject itself; the exterior one regards the objects in space as our imagination of them, their proximity and plurality. Böhme explains that in this sense Kant does not bring to the foreground our physical presence at the place of the perception, but he is considering rather our representation[6] of space – since he is calling space the separation or vicinity of objects that can belong to different places (places that are exterior to each other), and which could belong therefore to a common space, only by our representation of them. In this way space, for Kant, becomes a medium of representation.

Böhme explains further that, according to Kant, things are apparitions as long as their connections to each other are represented as a spatial connection in the medium of space. The relations between events are spatial relations to which the dimension of time has been added. Relations are recognizable primarily through their representation in space; therefore, they are then spatial models. The consequence of this is that the moment of representation comes into being through representation *in space*.

The space of physical presence, on the other hand, which is the space of daily experience, is considered by Böhme (2004: 133) to be fundamentally subjective. He understands experience always in self-reference. The physical space is the space through which for a subject the other becomes present. Therefore it is a space of action, a space of perception and, at the same time, a space of atmosphere, which is of great importance for Böhme. The physical space as a space of action, Böhme explains, is experienced as a playground, as a space of possibility for the subject and can be, at the same time, concrete and abstract (for example as social space). The space becomes for the acting subject the sphere of his immediate acts (Böhme 2004: 134). The space from the perspective of the 'I' position does not define the nature of the space itself, but the 'how' of the existence of the subject.

Virtual space is forcing, for Böhme, a differentiation between the space of physical presence and the space of medial representation. Virtual spaces are for him images, two or more dimensional media, in which a multiplicity comes into representation (Böhme 2004: 139). Böhme draws attention to the fact that virtual spaces cannot be called virtual solely because the things represented are fictive, or because they simulate realities, since this simulation is nothing but representation. According to Böhme, a space is virtual when a space of representation intertwines with the space of physical presence (Böhme 2004: 139). Put in another way, spaces of representation can be virtual spaces when they can be experienced as spaces of physical presence. Virtual spaces do not represent merely an overlapping of a space of physical presence with patterns of representation. They are not limited to these patterns of representation, are not necessarily close to reality, and the virtual presence in spaces of representation can be of an arbitrary structure (Böhme 2004: 140).

Virtual reality is, for Böhme, not understandable from the perspective of what it represents, and can also not be understood from the point of view of how it represents. The fact that a reality belongs to the domain of fiction, and that it simulates a reality which it does not incorporate itself, does not make a reality virtual. For Böhme, virtual reality is a reality that incorporates a fictive dimension that can be experienced physically. Virtual space is a fictional space with which a subject shares a physical presence and experience.

Böhme relates virtuality to the moment of its experience in the present. He is taking as an example a virtual that is digitally produced and can be experienced through connecting to technical devices, so he defines the virtual as a fiction that can be experienced physically.

Böhme's approach is paradigmatic for the early digital age, when this understanding of the virtual as fiction experienced physically through technical means of immersion became a consistent tradition in the philosophy of the digital media. Nevertheless later approaches detach the virtual from fiction and tend to perceive it as a reality. On the other hand, as in the works described here, the physical experience is not necessarily connected to sensory experience. The access of the viewer to the experience of a virtual reality is connected in these works with a conceptual tradition of reception. The viewer is physically participating in the work, but his conceptual (and not primarily sensorial) input is essential for his access to the work's reality.

In his early work, 'Artists Space Project' (2005), Carlos Bunga shows an empty space in which a series of polaroids, almost hidden, reveal a space-filling cardboard construction that had occupied that same space at a different time. The physical interference of the viewer with this real, but not actual, space determines that the viewer can actualize in his reception a past or future hypostasis of the work, which is only virtually there, but suggested through a specific display. The physical presence of the audience and its conceptual contribution to the work is, therefore, an essential condition of the possibility of the work, as Bunga affirms in the interview on page 39.

For Taguchi, a conjunction of relations is essential for the access to the virtual space. He comments upon this spatial intensity in an interview with Naokin, published in the Japanese journal *Tokyo Art Beat*.

> It's all about relationships basically, between things and people, people and people and so on. I haven't published it anywhere else but I do have a concept which guides all my artistic activity regardless of the material I'm using or the context I'm presenting the work: 'to intentionally induce spontaneously-generated relationships that emerge between all things'.
>
> (Matsuyama 2007)

In his various works, Gilles Deleuze (1994, 2007) explains the virtual as a potential reality that does not belong

Fig. 1.12: Yukihiro Taguchi, Cave, 2010,
Galeria aM.2, Tokyo, ©Yukihiro Taguchi.

Fig. 1.13: Yukihiro Taguchi, Cave, 2010,
Galeria aM.2, Tokyo, ©Yukihiro Taguchi.

to the immediate present. His definition puts forward a concept of virtuality that, unlike the virtual connected to the digital world, is understood by him as something real, and is not regarded as being a mere simulation of reality. Virtuality is, for him, a presence that has not been actualized yet, although it stays in the proximity of our material actuality.[7]

The differentiation that Gilles Deleuze is making between the virtual and the possible is essential; it is the differentiation between the actualization of the virtual and the realization of the possible. Gilles Deleuze cites extensively and comments on the work of Henri Bergson, whom he considers the great thinker of duration, multiplicity and virtuality. In his line of thought Deleuze states (Deleuze 2007) that the possible is correlated to the real: the possible is that which is expressed in the real and that which will transform into the real. It is concurring with the real, like a plan, which can be materialized. The real is therefore close to the possible, but it is also a limitation of the possible. The rapport between reality and possibility is set in opposition by Deleuze to the relationship between virtuality and actuality. The actual does not resemble the virtual in any way. Although the virtual is real, it does not have any actuality in the present. The actual does not limit the virtual and does not select what could become material from it, as happens in the possible-real model (Deleuze 2007: 120).

The actual is connected with the virtual through difference and divergence, which are understood by Deleuze as a form of creation. The transition from the virtual as a point of departure, and the actual as an endpoint, takes place through difference. This difference cannot appear in the domain of the possible; its apparition is connected to the virtual, since the possible is limited by the real and does not permit the appearance of the unexpected. In this sense virtuality belongs to a past that did not get consumed by the process of its transformation, and to a future that cannot be anticipated. Relationships in which the present is not predetermined by the past, and which result from unexpected configurations and ramifications, are the domain of difference for Deleuze. As far as virtuality exists, it has a reality that, even though it is not actual, has the power to be productive. On the other hand, difference cannot exist without actuality. The idea of virtuality brings into question the potentiality of different, differentiated forms of presence that Deleuze calls essentially positive and creative (Deleuze 2007: 128).

Deleuze formulates a distinction in this regard between differentiation and differenciation:

We call the determination of the virtual content of an Idea differentiation; we call the actualization of that virtuality into species and distinguished parts differenciation. It is always in relation to a differentiated problem or to the differentiated conditions of a problem that a differenciation of species and parts is carried out, as though it corresponded to the cases of solution of the problem. It is always a problematic field which conditions a differenciation within the milieu in which it is incarnated. Consequently – and this is all we wish to say – the negative appears neither in the process of differentiation nor in the process of differenciation. The Idea knows nothing of negation. The first process is identical with the description of a pure positivity, in the form of a problem to which are assigned relations and points, places and functions, positions and differential thresholds which exclude all negative determination and find their source in the genetic or productive elements of affirmation. The other process is identical with the production of finite engendered affirmations which bear upon the actual terms which occupy these places and positions, and upon the real relations which incarnate these relations and these functions. Forms of the negative do indeed appear in actual terms and real relations, but only in so far as these are cut off from the virtuality which they actualize, and from the movement of their actualization.

(Deleuze 1994, 207)

As Adrian Parr, a critic of Deleuze, explains, differentiation, originally a mathematical concept, is for Deleuze an open system in which new connections and directions are continually produced (Parr 2005: 75–76). What is differentiated is intensities and heterogeneous qualities. Differentiation happens only in the realm of the virtual. Differentiation is a process of continuous dividing and combining and it represents a creative flow. This creative movement and transformation is also what makes the virtual real, although not actual. Differenciation, on the contrary, represents the moment of the actualization of the virtual. This actualization can be either material or conceptual.

The difference about which Deleuze speaks is a net of relations, which appears through unpredictable configurations and in which the present is not predetermined by the past. As long as it exists as such, virtuality has a reality that has the power to be performative, productive. Its effect generates difference and divergence from the lived actuality.

The question that results is why differenciation does not become a system of representation and does not flow into similarity and identity. Deleuze explains that the actualization of the virtual has to be understood as a system that is exposed continuously to transformation. Differenciation is not to be understood as a version/a transposition of the virtual, which it differentiates, since it manifests through the appearance of creativity and the new. The processes of differenciation are for Deleuze not processes of identity, but of variation, of constant transformation. Differenciation does not mark a change of what already exists virtually, but reveals something fundamentally new in the process through which the virtual differentiates – that is through which it is actualized (Parr 2005: 75–76).

Bergson's thoughts regarding temporality are extended by Deleuze in the domain of space. The temporal model that Bergson elaborates is in the form of a net, where linearity of temporal expansion is abandoned in favour of heterogeneity and multiplicity. The past coexists with the present in a latent state, in other words, in a state of virtuality. Bergson's paradoxical formulations depart from duration, understood as a unitary temporality, in which the past, the future and the present form with other types of durations a net of connections and transformations (Deleuze 2007: 10). A virtual, latent temporality is always in dialogue with a dynamic, actualized temporality. They condition each other and none of them can be reduced to the other.

As results from the following group of interviews, conceiving and constructing a work along these dialogic temporal and spatial coordinates can push the work to surpass pre-programmed possibilities, in the sense of outreaching its constructed actuality. The role of the work's performative expression in the experience of the virtual is essential in this process. Understood as such, virtuality is the potential of the creative performance/act that each work manifests, and which brings excess, singularity and renovation. In Deleuze's words: the work is constantly actualized, as it is differentiated. The artists explain how each of them works with the qualities of a work that they do not conceive as having a fixed identity, but as resulting from the transformations that form suffers in time. •

Interviews

Interview with Carlos Bunga, October 2007

Q: From which initial questions did you start working with destruction and construction processes? Was it initially an architectural work or did you reach architecture through painting that you actually studied and that you continue to practice?

C.B.: I saw many buildings that collapsed in Portugal due to lack of maintenance and then I did some paintings and put them, as originals, directly onto the buildings and started to follow what was happening to them, what marks were left on them, like the buildings that started to show some signs of time, since deterioration is a sign of time. Then I started to take pictures.

I work with ephemerality and fragility and the processes connected to them, and photography for me is about that. I wanted to follow these processes in connection to space, and I started to do small objects first from paper and cardboard, and I painted them to give a more sculptural feeling. I have passed from these small objects to making big ones. These objects were a way to study the possibilities of space. You feel you could enter into them, but actually you can't, and it is this ambiguity, as a quality of space, in which I was interested. I was also interested in the models of architects and I thought how about you could enter into these models. These models are very interesting to me because they have a certain latent, unexpressed space possibility. My work is also about a projection of an idea about space, a possibility of space in a domain of the possible. That is why I see my later works also as models, although they have huge dimensions and can be entered. They can be regarded in this sense as prototypes of a process, as developments of an idea. While working with architecture that connects to a given building, like building over an already built form, I intend to suggest a new possibility for this particular space.

Q: What is the position of the human in architecture for you and how does your audience perceive its role in relation to your constructions?

C.B.: When I make these spaces, they are for me abstract spaces. Each of the people that go inside feel the space in a different way: an architect will feel it in one way, an artist in another, but they all have their experience of the space. On the contrary what I try to make is an abstract space, which can produce not just one experience, as people experiment with it, but a plurality of different spaces; different possibilities of thinking about space.

Q: Please describe in more detail this pluri-potential conceptual space. How do you actually make it happen, how do people interact with it, what are its qualities?

C.B.: What is important for me is the idea of *accelerated temporality*. For me the role of cardboard intervenes here. The irony is that as a very fragile and perishable material, I use it to build huge constructions. When I build and then destroy what I built, I actually accelerate in time the processes, in which a space is involved,

Fig. 1.14: Carlos Bunga, Landscape, 2011, Site specific installation, Hammer Museum, Los Angeles, ©Hammer Projects: Carlos Bunga, Photography ©Brian Forrest.

Fig. 1.15: Carlos Bunga, Milton Keynes
Project, 2006, Site specific installation,
Milton Keynes Gallery, Milton Keynes,
UK, ©Carlos Bunga.

like any cataclysms or natural disasters, which suddenly change the temporality of an environment. By destroying with my body the construction I have made, I accelerate the temporality of this space. In a new building this temporality is not as obvious as in an old building. When I use fragile cardboard for big constructions, and destroy it afterwards, I make an intervention in this temporality, I create a new temporality from the given possibilities.

In my work in 'Manifesta 5' in San Sebastian, I covered the entire interior exhibition space with cardboard, including the roof, and added colours after that to integrate the construction more into the space. After building it by hand for four weeks, my performance at the opening consisted of taking a knife and cutting the walls at the point where the wall meets the floor, from the inside out, while the building started to collapse in on me. In this project the people do not enter the construction, but they see the building collapse and this causes an intense feeling because I am there inside it myself. My work is mainly about fragility, but I also have an obsession with documentation, which seems to be a contradiction.

Usually after I've finished a project, I do some drawings of the space. These drawings are like sketches, but they come after. They are not documentation in the sense of recording a reality, because when I do a drawing, I change what really happened initially in the space. If these constructions are models, then they are making visible an idea, and these small document drawings I do afterwards are a way to document the possibilities that this installation created, and the many ideas that it carries latently. With this fake documentation, I intend to continue its potentialities. In my 2006 solo exhibition in the Milton Keynes Gallery in London, I did many drawings alongside the installation, but I didn't exhibit them that time. In the installation itself, I have explored its different possibilities: I didn't collapse the building, but I gave the impression that the building could collapse at any time, because I slightly cut all the walls at the point where the wall meets the floor and maintained a feeling of uncertainty and ambiguity about the fact that it could collapse at any moment. In my drawings I can, for example, simulate this collapsing and extract a possibility from that space. My drawings show processes that could happen with space.

I am also making architectural interventions in photography. In 2007, I was invited to work in a bank at the Justus Lipsius Building in Brussels, but the space was too big to intervene directly. So I took pictures of the space, made interventions in the photos and then exhibited the photographs in the same space, at the same place and from the same perspective that they were taken.

Q: Your work is also unfolding in a processual way. It is actually you who generates and conducts the transformations of space. How do you keep this balance between individual gestures and your own performance with space and the neutrality of these spatial experiments that represent what space can do, in a perspective that is independent of specific/particular human acts? Describe please your working process in this respect.

C.B.:   Normally I go to the gallery, I analyse the existing space and then I start to build. I don't know what will happen exactly and I try not to pre-conceive the course that the work will take, but I have a general concept. I see my constructions as paintings. The space is virgin, white like a canvas, and the way I put the elements in it is like the process of painting, adding elements to make a composition in space. That's why I like the work of Kurt Schwitters, because he also studied painting like I did, and I think the process through which he did 'Merzbau' is a painting process, but using the space. My initial small cardboard constructions were more regarding the idea of house, but now I work more on the concept of space. This makes a very big difference: a house is something more intimate, space is more abstract. It has more possibilities, potentialities, which can be suggested as such. My work is about appropriation of existing spaces and I think, for example, light is a form of appropriation of space. I do not work with artificial light inside the installation, but I use the existing light. Light is also a part of the architecture and I try to make sculptures, architecture, with the light of spaces.

Q: How do you use absence, the empty space? What is its role in your work?

C.B.:   For instance, in my 'Artists Space Project' in 2005 in New York, where I kept the whole gallery space empty for the opening, I only showed a light box in the gallery corridor, with photos about the process of construction of an installation. Although the visitor saw an almost empty space, I didn't show images about the deconstruction processes of the construction that had been in the space, but just the traces of the deconstructed installation. No images about the deconstruction process, which took place before the opening, could be found. I am interested in this tension that people can feel between what they see in an image and what they see in the real time in which they are present in a gallery space. It seems that something is missing in the process, and this temporal ellipse is actually the object of my work: it is what people have to reconstruct. For me, it is important how the audience finds a new space between the existing space of the gallery and the space I am building. This is a space of possibility, of experience, but it is immaterial. The audience is pushed to construct for themselves mentally a process that can take different courses in the end. The space in-between the original space and the space after the construction have been collapsed (so apparently the two spaces are the same), but actually what we reach is a space of suspension, it is a 'possible space', in which there are just some traces of memory of it left (the photos). I want to play with these different variations of space. I intend to reach a versatile space.

    To get back to your question, it is very interesting for me to work in the manner of architects, with space in itself, not just to put things on a Christmas tree. I also work with architectural elements and their spatial functions. In 2006, for the 'Miami Art Fair' I built a column, then I cut it, and I exhibited the rests that were left of it, naming it 'Pillar'. Also I made a corner, by rebuilding a corner of the stand in the same fair, and superimposed it on the existing corner.

Q: Why did you wish to concretely build the pillar, when you could have initially sculpted only a fragment/a rests of a column and still called it a pillar, since the concept would still work?

C.B.:   This process of building is important for me personally at the moment. Maybe in the future I will work in this way. I can do a fragmented building from the very beginning, but for me, constructing and destructing

Fig. 1.16: Carlos Bunga, Pillar, 2006, Miami Art Fair, ©Carlos Bunga.

is a process of understanding. That is why my work is site-specific. When someone is buying it, it cannot be removed from the place I exhibited it: it is just garbage, cardboard. Therefore I will have to go to his place and build it all over again. It is the same in retrospective exhibitions as well.

After I did the first performance of collapsing the construction in Manifesta 5 in San Sebastian, everybody wanted me to repeat that, but I didn't agree to it, because what I am doing is not a performance. I want to show something about the qualities of space, and not to do a show, in the sense of a personal performance, which is the staging of me as an individual. People started to cry after my performance at Manifesta, because the collapsing moment is very impressive, but for me this is not what I wanted to show. That is why I usually don't repeat this performance. I prefer to collapse the building before the opening, or I don't collapse it at all. I want to suggest exactly the opposite of a personal performance: I am interested in the different possibilities of the same space. My drawings or paintings are different variations that deepen my subject much more than this personal performance. Each project is a fragment of a broader dynamic.

    I appreciate the work of Chris Burden in which he is shooting himself in the arm. The moment of shooting is about sculpture, about transformation, as the collapsing of a building is, for me, a transformation of space. Other references for me are also the Gutai group, and Lucio Fontana, with his cuts in the canvas, even if it is more formal.

Q: The fact that your work can function on a path that is not predefined by you, and that it can develop and change further, independently, based on its internal principles, could make your objects very interesting from the point of view of design. They make a very important contribution in this direction, showing the possibility of an object to be pluri-contextual, to be able to adapt to its environment and to change its functions in time.

C.B.:   I am actually working with design, and my starting point is an investigation that I am doing now in the Vitra Museum – on chairs, in particular. I have inscribed the original name and year in my drawing for every chair from the Vitra collection. These chairs are like ghosts of the particular political and social contexts attached to every one of them. Very important for me in this respect is the appropriation of space in big installations, but also how domestic objects, for example, can change by appropriating qualities of their environment. The table in its old position has a usage. If I alter it and distort it in my installation, it will change our usual direction of thinking. The design of these chairs has a domestic dimension, which connects architecture with sculpture and art history, and all these allusions are not present in the big installations. In my work with the chairs, the problems that I addressed with the big installations are more contextualized, have different references.

Q: You mean that you work with the fact that these chairs make visible some new directions of thinking, which were emerging in the arts, through these everyday objects?

C.B.:   Yes. I am also interested in the relation between objects and social context. Like the collective memory, which a chair bears [...] which is also connected to the capacity of an object for multi-functionality. That is why many architects are also very interested in making furniture and experiment a lot with it. I like to provoke the question: what is this object actually? Is it a table, it is an architectural model? And then you start to think about it.

Q: The idea of maximizing the potential of an object or building until it loses the possibility of concrete realization, is it connected for you also with the idea of utopia?

C.B.:   Words like *between*, *utopia*, even *model* are very abstract concepts; their content of information can be very complex. When we use them we rely in a very formalist way on them, that is why I also can hardly use them without re-formulating their content. For me it is very important not to capture a meaning, but to let meanings interconnect, to capture also the potentiality of these concepts.

Interview with Yukihiro Taguchi, January 2008

Q: Your position in relation to your own work (be it video or performance) is ambiguous: you seem to deny your auctorial position, deleting retroactively all the traces of your involvement from the end-form of the work. How would you describe your own creative process in this case? How do you approach your own role as an author?

Y.T.: I am for my work, what is called in the traditional Japanese theatre, a kuroko: a character, all dressed in black (his face is covered too), who leads the entire piece from the backstage, who prepares the stage, who gives directions to the actors and sometimes appears on the stage, but always stays unnoticed. Without his presence in the background the piece could not advance. Still he has to stay always hidden, even though he appears in the foreground. This is the best position that I could take for my work. If I mingle too much with my work, then I will make a work about myself. But what I intend is keeping the work as work always in the foreground. My work exists only with the presence of the audience, without them my work would not be possible. I wish that the audience acts inside my work, without me commanding their role in this process, whereas both of us (me and the audience) could be actors on one and the same level. One of my strategies for this is also uploading my films and the documentation of my work on YouTube. Everyone can re-use my works as any other material, and appropriate it according to their will.

I choose the term *kuroko* since I do not wish to intervene in my work; the work should not show something about myself, but about itself.

Q: What is exactly the role of the audience in configuring the work?

Y.T.: My work is an attempt to connect people. I try to create empty spaces that give to the visitors an alternative possibility in which they can experience together time and space. Conflict and danger can be parts of it as well, since they create an enhanced experience of the real in the exceptional situation, in which provisional communities are formed during the performances.

Q: What do you consider to be the difference between performances nowadays and the avant-garde performance art of the 1960s and 1970s?

Y.T.: As I see it, in the avant-garde the audience and the performer played separate roles, whereas now this distance between the two is neutralized.

Q: Why do you call many of your installations *performative,* and in what way do you understand this term? How would you differentiate between the terms 'performance' and 'performativity'?

Y.T.: For me installations or performances are paintings. I see them as three-dimensional painting processes, and I am interested in the way in which a certain composition of colours, for example, changes the nature and the appearance of each of its components. In a certain chromatic composition, blue is blue. In another one, it is not blue any more. The situation changes and the meaning is dislocated as well. I investigate these

Fig. 1.17: Yukihiro Taguchi, Giftplatz 2, 2007, Performance, Mauerpark, Berlin, ©Yukihiro Taguchi.

processes in space, as well as the capacity of space to generate them. We usually compress, extend, construct our own time and space from separate moments, and thus we ignore its linear continuity, creating our own specific micro spatial-temporal configurations.

My film in Sarajevo, 'Visitor' (2007), shows a situation in which these spatio-temporal superpositions become evident. The tourists that stayed near the fire monument had all been in the same spot in different temporal moments, and photographed the same monument from the same perspective. This multiple superposition has a continuity of its own and creates a space that is different from that experienced by each visitor. I was interested here in this over-layering of experience in relation to space. The space that results is a performative space, in the sense that it realizes itself in a performance. I regard architecture from the point of view of this spatial performance that is more than a sum of the experience of the various persons that contributed with their actions to a certain space in time.

In this situation in which we have gathered for this discussion, we share a certain time and space, but when you go, another time and space will come for you and another will come for me. I am trying to analyse these processes from the point of view of the space, and not from certain personal experiences. I therefore do not stage my own performance, but I try to capture the transformations that space generates.

Q: Your works can be seen in this case also as a documentation of this spatial performance? What is then for you the role of documentation in the creation of experience?

Y.T.:   I consider documentation as being a work in its own right. It is an experiment with reality and can be, as well, considered performative.

Interview with Noam Braslavsky, July 2008[8]

Q: As you yourself work with space, both as a gallerist and visual artist in your own works, please describe your understanding of Yukihiro Taguchi's employment of space.

N.B.:   Yuki is using space in the same particular way in which he is using situations. He needs little and he always makes interesting readings of what he finds in space. Maybe it is the Japanese space that he is used to, a narrow space, in which probably the private space and its density is also defined in a different way. In his works this inner private space of air, or the space between people, is mainly a social space. For example, his works where he is wrapping people or objects up is not packing in the way Christo is doing it. Taguchi is wrapping up momentary situations and their social dimension. On the other hand, I think that Yuki does not deal with the concrete relationship between man and space, but rather with the idea of space and a virtual space that is important for him. He is not evoking other spaces, but works with spaces that *could* exist. He is also concerned with borders, creating borders that are invisible, or that actually do not exist. His borders and spaces exist virtually, and he is showing the possibility of these virtual spaces. Taguchi is packing all that a situation can carry: not the concrete space between two objects, but a virtual space of meaning that exists mentally. A space that is wrapping three people in nylon can be an aggressive space, but it is a *virtually* aggressive space. So in his work, he is turning this virtual space into a real space in order to show it.

I started working with Yuki due to his capacity to improvise. He uses and appropriates that which already exists, and brings a system to space. Suddenly the space is his, due to the new definition that he applied to it. He does not redefine spaces in the customary way, by sound and light, or by a certain use of material, but only by his new definition of a place. He not only created a new order, in the sense of something new, but he created *movement*. Throughout the history of culture, people have always ordered spaces, they have standardized spaces and the spaces that we encounter around us recall these spatial paradigms. Yuki works very precisely, but without the effect of quoting such patterns that could have a remembrance effect.

Interview with Daniel Lima, July 2008[9]

Q: How did you first start to work with Yukihiro Taguchi? What interested you in his work?

D.L.:   The first installation of his that I saw was one in which he packed a lot of rubbish that he found in the basement of a gallery in plastic. The plastic was hanging in the air like a wave. I thought initially that he transformed space just with what he found in it, to magnify all the rubbish. I understood later, working with him, that he uses the space for itself, in itself, with itself. In his work 'Moment' (2007)[10] he conceived of a game with space, changing the installation every day. For me, his approach to architecture changes its nature, from being connected to permanency, into a construction that results from the involvement of various media, since his architecture results from a series of pictures that he takes after every movement and that he composes into a film. He is working with what is nearest to him, with the most obvious. He is materializing

Fig. 1.18: Yukihiro Taguchi, Stamm_Berlin, 2007, Berlin, ©Yukihiro Taguchi.

the unseen space, he is materializing the absence, distracting the space and building, at the same time, another space. He is constructing absence and also working with stuff that is absolutely evident, but that we cannot see. There are artists that are engaged politically, but there are others, including Yuki, who are preoccupied with the art market, with social issues, but without expressing it literally. Also he is not doing his art literally: it is *as if* he is doing art. I could say that he is almost not producing art, but rather making obvious a way to see life, a way to live. It is the audience, rather, who interprets his work as art. Other artists provide an interpretation with their work. Yuki, on the contrary, keeps the work open and it can be filled with meaning. The process is similar with his working method: the show constructs itself. And Yuki discovers space by creating it, while the audience becomes integrated in the work.

But he is also playing with beautiful shapes and plastic constructions, with sculptural and architectural allusions, which are visually attractive and full of references. It is another game of his.

Q.:   'Performatives Spazieren'[11], 2008, was the title of the show that extended 'Moment' from the gallery into the open space of Kreuzberg. The concept of performativity is an integral part of his work and he uses this term to name his processual work. What do you consider that it designates exactly, and why does it define his approach?

D.L.:   *Performative* is definitely not referring to his performance, which is a physical *component* of his work. The gallery was open from 3 to 8 pm, so people could see him from 3 to 5 pm working for the construction of an installation from the gallery's wood panels that changed every day, in other words: performing. But he is actually not delivering a performance: the goal is erecting the construction. His work is *performative*, maybe, because it is always changing. His animations are *performative* also, as they show the work moving and transforming in time and space. And I would consider his work to be *performative,* because he is the work itself, but he never appears in it.

Others artists that I represent are manifesting their descent from conceptual art and from various traditions of thought. But for Yuki I never see this necessity as his work does not represent a certain tradition. It doesn't take much understanding of his work to connect him with Gordon Matta Clark, for example. There are formal affinities. When he placed the wood panels on the grass in the Bethanien garden, he thought it looked like Carl Andre, but then he realized it didn't, because the pieces moved and therefore it was completely different.

For Yuki, constructing can be a painting; the installation looks like a painting, or the process of construction can be a painting process, in the sense that painting is an organization of space, a construction with colours. In a similar way his videos, in which many hours of walking materialize in a three-minute video, are self-contained pieces, but are not documenting other works.

NOTES

1   As an example, Derrida (1988) is mentioning the signature.
2   In her article, Bal (2009) explores connections between the uniqueness of the presence that performativity generates, and the cultural memory that a performance presupposes.
3   The term 'processuality' (which is used by Carlos Bunga himself) signifies a row of processes that are suffered by an environment.
4   The term 'spatiality' (also utilized by Carlos Bunga himself) will be used in this volume to designate not a concrete space, but the idea of space and space in general.
5   Excerpt from the press release of 'Marxitecture' (2009) in Gallery Krome.
6   *Anschaaung* is the German term that Böhme uses.
7   For the relationship of Deleuze's work with contemporary arts, see Krogh Jensen (2001) and Grosz (2001).
8   Noam Braslavsky was the director of the Berlin gallery GDK (Galerie der Kuenste) where Taguchi showed 2008 his exhibition 'Ordnung'. The gallery closed in 2009.
9   Daniel Lima was the founder and gallerist of Air Garten, in Berlin Kreuzberg. The gallery closed in 2010. Yukihiro Taguchi showed in 2007 his work 'Moment' and 2008 'Moment. Performatives Spazieren' in this gallery.
10 'Moment', 2007, was the first exhibition by Yukihiro Taguchi in Air Garten.
11 Spazieren (German: to stroll).

CHAPTER 2
Palimpsest: Deconstructed architecture and the idea of the ruin

Deconstructivism from its sources

Jacques Derrida's writings on architecture, and his collaboration with various architects, had a material outcome in the so-called 'deconstructivist' architectural style developed in the 1980s. Its protagonists Bernard Tschumi, Peter Eisenman, Frank Gehry, Zaha Hadid or the group Coop Himmelblau found a concretization for the philosophical teachings of Derrida and transposed them, under Derrida's initial supervision, programmatically into a new alphabet of forms. Concomitant with the planned development of a deconstructivist architecture, in art, various experiments had been made that searched for a more performative architecture, one that incorporates the event.

The works described here, and many other recent experiments in installation art that deal with construction processes and built space, formulate an understanding of architecture that offers realizations and solutions to the revolutionary thinking of Derrida about architecture, while bringing it, some decades later, into convincing material form. I intend to show in the following that – in a different way than the modus operandi of the architectural discipline itself – recent conceptual works have found ways in which architecture can accomplish the philosophical project of Derrida. These conceptual installations subsume performance, and even result from movement, transformation and, very often, from the choreography of its 'users'. These types of works have realized in practical terms what Derrida calls a 'non-Heideggerian' architecture, which will be explored in the following pages.

In many of his texts and interviews, Derrida underlines that deconstruction cannot become a technique in architecture, and most of all it should not consist of de-constructing something already built. Deconstruction has for him its own rhetoric, which dictates no formal precepts and is not connected to a discipline, but on the contrary should introduce a new way of thinking.

Deconstructivism started with Derrida's preoccupation with intertextuality, which is based on an affinity between text and spatial configuration. Writing is for Derrida an espacement, a term used throughout his work and which designates the release of time and space through dislocation from previous structures. Similarly, what Derrida calls the *archi-écriture* is also a way to write space, to make space for a certain event (Derrida and Meyer 1997: 319–323).

Constructions like 'Folie' in Parc de la Villette (a practical as well as theoretical collaboration between Derrida and Tschumi), the private houses (House I–IV, House X) or the 'Fin D'Ou T Hou S' of Peter Eisenman, manifest a disjunction in style: the fragment gains stylistic autonomy, the elements are opposed and juxtaposed into the body of the construction.[1] The private houses of Peter Eisenman were seen as a borderline of architecture: they are extremely provocative visually but are also completely non-functional and absurd.

Derrida pleads for an architecture that is not necessarily subjected to the function of living, but rather one that steps out of Heidegger's concept of 'dwelling' and becomes a conceptual experiment. Deconstruction is not meant to remove something that's already been built (in a concrete or cultural sense) in order to make space for a domain that could be 'cultivated' again. Derrida's search, for that which he calls a 'non-Heideggerian constructing and dwelling' (Derrida 1989a: 74), is the search for an architecture that does not find its finality in something outside itself, but which also does not propose a nihilistic form of habitation, which would search to restore a 'pure', 'original' architecture. The point would be rather to encounter an architecture that could be *correlated with other media and other arts.*

With the concepts of *trans-architecture* and *an-architecture* Derrida designates an architecture that exists only through the presence of an audience, as an essential condition of its existence. Architecture is not an existing space to be filled, but it emerges with the presence of its users. An-architecture is the place of this dynamic undermining of the tectonic and housing qualities of architecture. Trans-architecture is a medium not for offering to the user, observer, aesthete and consumer a work to be consumed, but to make him *meet* the work, to invent it and to maintain it in the present ('maintenant l'architecture') (Derrida 1997b: 324–336, section 9).

In his discussion with Christopher Norris, Derrida defines deconstructivism as 'something that is more hidden, more relevant, less approachable for a system or a method, it is that which makes this thematic deconstructivism in the discourse, in teaching and in the art possible' (Derrida 1989a: 75).

Taken as architectural provocations, the ideas of Derrida were finding a visual outcome that resulted in situations in which architecture could not be lived in: no access to the bed, holes in the floor of the living room and stairs leading to nowhere (especially in the 'Houses' of Peter Eisenman). In an interview with Charles Jencks, Eisenman defends his work and refers to the necessity of attacking the given with all its sets of representation. The conquest of a new concrete, cultural and social territory is for Eisenman a condition for the realization of the new (Eisenman 1989: 141–149). In these extreme works that follow quite literally the precepts of Derrida, functionality is rather negated then reformulated, and this *formal* negation established a style that finally inverted the initial project of Derrida – that of finding an architecture that surpasses its function and its formal determination. What became an architectural style in the 1980s can be best followed through the exhibition curated by Eisenman and Philip Johnson in 1989 in the Museum of Modern Art, New York, and dedicated to the past decade of deconstructivist architecture.[2] The exhibition collected the most representative pieces of this period, and contributed to fixing in formal terms the characteristics of the so-called deconstructivist style in architecture. It unified and classified the works under the criteria of a common formal apparatus, a temporal appurtenance, and chose some exemplary pieces that embodied the essential features of this style.

Nevertheless Derrida speaks of deconstructivism*s* in order to stress the heterogeneity of the concept (Derrida 1989a: 71–75) and that it does not belong to a certain period of time. Deconstruction has been formulated by Derrida rather as a conceptual attitude that does not define a style, a project, a critique or a program, but represents rather a way of thinking that can be identified with different artists in different time periods. Derrida gives the example of René Magritte and his interlacing of text and image.

As for him architecture is the writing of space, Derrida uses the term *espacement* to designate the creation through architecture of a dimension for the event, the creation of a 'constructional event' – a scenography of the transition, which invents a place, which does not overlast through the stability of his affirmation, but by 'sequence, open seriality, narrativity, the kinematic, dramaturgy, choreography' (Derrida 1997b: 324-336, section 3). In his discussion with Christopher Norris, Derrida affirms that deconstructivism cannot be seen as a phenomenon of Modernism, and even less so of Postmodernism. It is for him a certain way to think:

> Deconstructivism is not only a technique of an architect that knows how he can deconstruct something that has been already constructed. From here we can pass to what deconstruction connects to writing: its space, thinking as a path, the opening of a way, which – without knowing where it leads – leaves its traces.
>
> (Derrida and Meyer 1997: 319–323)

Deconstruction, its concrete outcomes and the arts

The 1994 volume *Deconstruction and the Visual Arts: Art, Media, Architecture* (Brunette and Wills 1994) contains an interview by the editors with Derrida. Derrida talks here about the fact that deconstruction is a way of withstanding the authority of philosophical discourse. Therefore it cannot be understood simply as a method that can be applied in the analysis of a text (if it is artistic or filmic, for example). On the contrary, the text appears in the moment in which deconstruction comes into play in various aspects and domains. Discourses (and *espacement* implies a discourse) are included in every work. Derrida also mentions that the application of deconstruction in the domain of art is more legitimate than its application in the domain of text, since it performs in its essence a resistance against the authority of logocentrism.[3] We can understand from here that deconstruction in art represents a modality of creating a body of work that is placed outside the hegemony of a pre-formulated discourse and functions as a condition of emergence of the event that induces creation and invention.

Approaches to architecture coming from visual and performative arts, like the ones presented in this volume, have specific tools that expand the identity of the built form, in a way that the discipline itself did not materialize in this form. Architecture results here from including the event in the body of architecture, introducing movement into its experience and reception, mingling construction with deconstruction processes, corroborating the built form with various other media, and conceiving of the audience/user as an essential condition of the existence of architecture.

In the performances of Hironari Kubota, for example, architecture emerges from an amalgamation of vestiges from different contexts and times: spinning his industrial sculptural objects, he is dismantling and decomposing them, until they are shown to be containers of meanings imprinted culturally in specific forms. His moving, hybrid architectures result from digging for a historic space connected to his own experience in Japanese popular religious festivals and from reminiscences of a contemporary, already consumed industrial patrimony. These architectural forms that emerge ephemerally during his performances are enacted, almost ritualistically, by the audience (Kubota 2011 interview).

Derrida not only stresses that the architectural work cannot be understood without the existence of its users, but he also affirms that it cannot exist without them. At the same time, his vision of architecture is not that of an abode, a home, but should be conceived rather as an undermining of the tectonic influences of architecture. An-architecture is one that surpasses its functions of habitation, its function as Heidegger's concept of 'dwelling'.

In the arts, architecture that results from or is perceivable as an event progressively developed and came close to Derrida's idea. Unlike the systematic creation of a deconstructivist architecture that came from the discipline of architecture itself, in the arts a multi-media approach, the inclusion of movement, and a factor of unexpectedness in the body of architecture contributed to the formation of an 'architecture of the event'. From the early works of Gordon Matta-Clark in the mid-seventies, to the recent works of Rafael Lozano-Hemmer using various media and devices, architecture is, by its essence, not subordinated to the function of dwelling, and exists only through interaction.

Regarding his project 'Choral Works' with the architects Peter Eisenman and Bernard Tschumi in Parc de la Villette, Derrida describes the nature of a deconstructive artistic work as an ideatic palimpsest with no hierarchy, which gains its meaning through permeability of its structuring processes:

> Now, this structure of the non-totalizable palimpsest which draws from one of its elements the resources for the others (their *carriere* or quarry), and which makes an unrepresentable and unobjectifiable labyrinth out of this play of internal differences (scale without end, *scaling* without hierarchy): this is precisely the structure of *Choral Works*.
>
> (Derrida 1997b: 325)

In 'Why Peter Eisenman writes such good books' (Derrida 1997a: 336–347) Derrida writes:

> For all these layers of meaning and forms, of visibility and invisibility extend (lie as in layers) *into* each other, *on* or *under* each other, *in front of* or *behind* each other, but the truth of the relationship is never established, never stabilized in any judgement. [...] In this abyssal palimpsest, no truth can establish itself on any primitive or final presence of the meaning.
>
> (Derrida 1997b: 325)

Fig. 2.1: Yukihiro Taguchi, Moment, 2009, 5th Vento Sul Biennial, Curitiba, Brasil, ©Yukihiro Taguchi.

In the same article describing the Choral Works, he affirms:

> Like the work it names, the title Choral Works is at the same time palimpsest and labyrinth, a maze of superimposed structures. […] And the structure of our title obeys the same law; it has the same form of potentiality, the same power: the dynamics of an immanent invention.

(Derrida 1997a: 341)

Recent architectural practice has been dominated by a vision that does not restrict itself to a finished building as the object of the discipline, but has widened its borders to include open-ended practice and pure conceptual exercise, which is not defined causally and chronologically. The architectural group Coop Himmelblau, established in 1968 in Vienna, introduced the concept of liquid space in architectural theory. This new spatial understanding was meant to create a spatiality, in which no perspective and no position of the viewer could dominate the understanding of space. This 'democratic' configuration of space, which does not favour an authoritative positioning and possibly does not instrumentalize space, is a complex construction both on a spatial and a temporal level. The construction favours various perspectives concomitantly, and diverse moments of observation coexist. These plural layers in space prevent the performance space from being segregated into stage and audience space. This fluid space can therefore incorporate and make visible the passage of time (Dimendberg 1994: 175).

An understanding of time that is not based on the linear development of a construction from the initial idea to its concrete realization, but on oscillation and simultaneity, has emerged out of current complex historical frameworks and historiography. It also permeates the work of another group of architects: Herzog and De Meuron. Peggy Phelan (2002: 290–299) situates their work in a Freudian line of argumentation, which makes reference to the concomitant drive for life and death that motivates any development for Freud. Phelan describes a building as an organism with parts that either develop further or die, while other parts return to an earlier state in order to repeat the game of growth. In this light, contemporary architectural practice, whether a building, an installation or a performative gesture, started to be imagined as a conjunction of a multiplicity of possible solutions, beginning with the avant-garde and culminating in contemporary practice (Phelan 2002: 291). Phelan regards every connection between the development and the completion of a building as a form of performance. In the case of architects like Herzog and De Meuron, this performativity results from opening up architectonic space to media interventions. This group of architects included serialized photography or screen printing, for example, in the structure of a building.

The works of the artists discussed here also describe processes of dislocation. Elements of a system (social, urban etc.), or a structure (visual, architectonic), are detached from linear movement and immersed in foreign processes and thus break discourses of legitimacy. These works variate on a formal or aesthetic level, but they all share the conditions of the existence of the 'deconstructive' architectural work that Derrida describes. It is what Derrida called 'seriality', which has become a defining component of contemporary conceptual art. It invests architecture with a kinematic movement and with a subtle, but unpredictable dramaturgy, which results also from the interaction with its audience. In the work of Taguchi, for example, provisory architectures result from the repetition of the same movements. The 'stop-motion' technique from animation constructs and deconstructs a fixed time and space conjunction, from which an architecture based on an internal dynamic takes shape. The same thing happens with the shifted architectural frames of Cristian Rusu, which introduce time in the medium of drawing. Here the oscillation of a stable form creates an architecture that unfolds in time and destabilizes the values associated with the habitable and tectonic qualities of architecture and questions the historic authority of models and prototypes in architecture. Rusu's drawings formulate an architecture that doubts tradition as formal continuity and shakes the self-implied authority that architecture can exercise in a social context. A whole history of form is questioned by the simple pulsation of these paradigmatic forms.

From the interviews on pages 68–78 an understanding of the role of the audience can be extracted, which differentiates itself from the avant-garde's cooperation with the audience in the 'performing' of a 'participatory work'. In recent works the spectator is not only a co-author of the work, but the audience makes the *existence* of the work possible in the first place, as was stated by Derrida. The conceptual participation (and not necessarily a physical one, as practised in the avant-garde) makes the work exist. It is because the works are newly invented through their reception every time that (as Derrida affirms) they are always maintained in the present.

In Cristian Rusu's recent work, for example 'Project for a Modernist Pavilion' (2013), the reference to modernism is a polemic one. Presented at the Kunstraum Kreuzberg Bethanien, Berlin, he envisions this work as a melancholic meditation on urban space. He designed an urban pavilion from a replica of a concrete element of the Berlin Wall, building an open spatial structure that creates a leisure spot – a resting and meeting point in the middle of the urban rush. This piece of urban furniture is intended to offer an opportunity to ponder one's own immediate environment (in this case the traumatized and politically charged, divided city of Berlin). Although based on a formal element from 1961 (when the Berlin Wall started to be built), it recalls memories of modernist pavilions and constructivist forms with their early socialist aesthetic. This iconic element of recent German history, which progressively turned

Fig. 2.2: Cristian Rusu, Space Drawing 1, 2009, Drawing pencil on paper, ©Cristian Rusu & Galeria Plan B, Photo, ©Cristian Rusu.

Fig. 2.3: Cristian Rusu, Project for a Modernist Pavilion, 2013, Kunstraum Kreuzberg Bethanien, Berlin, ©Cristian Rusu, Photo, ©Viviana Druga.

into a touristic Berlin pop icon, is channelled in this work back to the still concealed and abstruse political territory that it occupied. In the dull ambience of the Berlin exhibition space, with the help of miniature wall elements, a video drafts possible variations of the pavilion, as well as its 'traces': dark grey stones are placed on the gallery floor and both block passage and mark imprints of the wall on the ground. Rough and dark, these stones bring to light again the tensions of a history not yet fully digested.

The role of performativity in deconstructivism

Derrida's deconstructivist architecture has been confronted with a critical perspective that stated that deconstruction is subsuming in a more timely shape, the same principle of the 'classical' architecture. As Derrida himself reports (1989a: 74), critics have argued that his theory of architecture corresponds in essence to the same Heideggerian function of habitation, which Derrida aims to avoid. Derrida sees the solution to this problem in the relocation of the question to another level: 'Because the question, that I am now posing, is not what they construct, but how we interpret, what they construct' (Derrida 1989a: 74).

In this sense, also, these works are especially relevant. They are usually not particularly innovative in their formal aspects. A 'house', a 'shelter' or a 'bus stop' (in the work of Sancho Silva) result from the way in which they are invested with meaning by their users. In this sense, not only the contribution of the artist, but also that of the 'reader' is equally important in the formation of the work. We are confronted less with actual buildings but we are offered an experience of architecture and what architecture can be.

Talking about an audience that is neither a spectator, nor a participant, Derrida calls the work a commitment, not only for those who create it, but also for those who are part of it, by thinking about it, and for those who are 'experiencing space differently':

> From this point of view I think that the architectural experience (let's call it that rather than talking about buildings as such) what they offer is precisely the chance of experiencing the possibility of these inventions of a different architecture, one that wouldn't be, so to speak, 'Heideggerian' […]
>
> (Derrida 1989a: 74)

> We will not reply by giving access to some final meaning, whose assumption would be finally promised us. No, it is justly [*justement*] a question of what happens to meaning: not in the sense of what would finally allow us to arrive at meaning, but of what happens to it, to meaning, to the meaning of meaning
>
> (Derrida 1997b : 324-336, section 4)

In his 'Fifty-Two Aphorisms for a Foreword' (Derrida 1989b: 67–72), which is itself an intertextual construction of conjunctive deliberations on text and architecture, Derrida analyses the conditions of the emergence of architecture. Regarding the term 'performative', Derrida writes:

> We understand by that (n.b. performativity) these moments where knowledge becomes work, when the theoretical statement no longer allows itself to be dissociated from the event called 'creation', 'composition', 'construction'. It is not sufficient to say that architecture is one of its best paradigms. Even the word and the concept of paradigm have an exemplary architectural value.
>
> (Derrida 1989b: 68, Aphorism 34)

The performative space can also be brought into relation with what Derrida calls the spatiality of the work. Derrida explains how the elements and layers that form a particular history of space, and remain inscribed in the space, can develop a meaning similar to that of a palimpsest, which can be absorbed in the act of its reception. Without predetermining the work, interpretation affirms and consolidates the work. Still, deconstruction is not seen by him as an interpretative method that can be applied to the work. The work appears in the moment at which it is deconstructed/interpreted, and cannot therefore be reduced to one of the various forms that it takes in the process of its transformation.

> Deconstruction is not simply forgetting the past. [...] The archive of these deconstructed structures should be as readable as possible.
>
> (Derrida 1989a: 73)

> Of the citation: even though it is engaged here according to a singular modality, even though it does not imitate in the manner of a painting or a sculpture that come to represent a model, the architecture of the 'tradition' belongs to the space of the *mimesis*. It is traditional; it constitutes the tradition by itself. Despite appearances the 'presence' of an edifice does not refer only to itself. It also repeats, signifies, evokes, convokes, reproduces and cites. It carries towards the other and refers to itself, it divides even in *reference*. [...]
>
> (Derrida 1989b: 67, Aphorism 13)

The *Architecture without Project* that Derrida delineates can be understood as performative being one that incorporates the *possibility* of the emergence of an enhanced event. It goes beyond a predictable event. The term 'Project' could be understood in this context as a programme, a manifesto that makes a prescription, and orientates the work towards a certain predictable finality.

> [...] To say that it does not have a project does not amount to denouncing its empiricism or its adventurism. In the same way an architecture without a project is engaged perhaps in a more thoughtful, more inventive,

more propitious work than ever came from the event.

(Derrida 1989b: 68, Aphorism 36)

Project is explained by Derrida at another point as:

> A project is something which is prior to the work, which has its own economy, a governing role which can then be applied and developed [...]. And you have the same kind of relation between the project, or the concept, and its carrying-out in practice as between, say, the transcendental signified and its incarnation on the body, in writing etc.

(Derrida 1989a: 74)

Performative reception (as event) and documentation

The question of the reception of work without a programme is discussed by Derrida in his book on painting: *Die Wahrheit in der Malerei/The Truth in Painting* (Derrida 1992). In this book, Derrida discusses the necessity of denying the presence of truth in the art object. Derrida describes every form of interpretation as a contamination with other media, which does not permit the totality of meaning to be contained always in the immediate presence of the object. The analytical approach to art loses therefore its claim of objectivity and neutrality in relation to other discourses and the object itself. Derrida sees every interpretation as a route that opens up the possibility of the emergence of successive or parallel interpretations. These are seen by him as events. The deconstruction of the unitary meaning of a work/text reveals a work as a fragment – the Trace, as Derrida designates it. This fragment, which can belong to different contexts of meaning, is not understood by him as a definitive statement, but as a principle of plurality.

Documentation is a means not only of reading, but also of (de)constructing architecture. Usually artists work with retrospective documentation, which includes a virtual dimension in the body of the work. This documentation, that is often related to previous aspects or possible hypostases of architecture that the artists treat, does not aim to reconstruct a materiality lost in time, but instead to formulate or follow a potential that a certain situation has shown and that has not been pursued in its actual material form. Documentation does not belong to the past, but can take place – as a potentiality – before, after or at the same time as the event. In this way a past, future or possible situation becomes part of the actuality of the viewer and is integrated into a new spatial and temporal continuity.

Carlos Bunga works with the ways in which reality can be re-assembled by shifting the moment *present* on the time scale, more so than with particular documents or particular events. His 2009 series of drawings 'Ruins Projects' departs from the 'Ruin', a work that he created in 2008 at Art Unlimited/Art Basel, and which serves as a foundation for later constructions, as it also represents the visible remains of a presumably anterior construction, which Bunga archaeologically releases through drawing from the subterranean. Bunga's drawings that alter past states of constructions, or his collection of newspapers announcing disasters or natural calamities, could seem to be a documentary practice par excellence. He is re-archiving an already archived event, one that has hitherto been transformed into information. But contrary to the usual archive material, his intervention reinvests the original event with its theatrical dimension. An expanded object is the result of his writings, drawings and the re-situating of this material into a personal register of meaning that re-negotiates, *oscillates*. This new record, unstable in its not clearly defined borders, marks a cumulative shift. It is at once part of a media archive (a newspaper for example), and part of a personal archive of meaning. It is enriched with incoherence, multiplicity and the incomprehensible – just like the original event itself.

As Bunga himself repeatedly affirms, he works with the potentialities that situations carry, rather than with the situations themselves. He therefore operates actually with what Jacques Derrida calls, using a grammatical term, 'the future anterior'.

'The archive as not being simply a recording of the past, but also something that is shaped by a certain power, a selective power, and shaped by the future, by the future anterior' (Derrida, J. 1998b; Hamilton, Vrene, Graeme 2002: 40). At another point, Jacques Derrida discusses the future anterior as a 'double desire for the past and the future' (Derrida, J. 1998b; Hamilton, Vrene, Graeme 2002: 40).

Bunga's personal archive with newspaper clippings of architectural disasters contains snapshots and headlines both from Portugal and abroad. Destruction is a constant interest of Bunga's, but it is conceived by him not as pure annihilation, but rather as a process of revealing hidden layers in the identity of an object. The moments of break and transformation push the objects into a development that could not be foreseen, and create hybrid objects that have an alienated identity. Bunga stresses that it is not a matter of destruction, but of *inversion*. This inversion converts processes of construction, and presents the 'possibility to deal in an abstract way with these constructions' (Bunga 2009 interview). Bunga works with a negative presence, a reverse documentation, of the evidence that he finds in time.

In Bunga's work destruction occurs not only during an event, but also the process of degradation is evident. It discloses, with its social and political origins, rotten infrastructures that Bunga implicitly amends in relation to the Portuguese reality. Taking into consideration the decay of historic architecture in Portugal, his drawings transmit a critical commentary on the public policy of conservation: monuments and protected historic buildings are uninhabited and simply collapse due to lack of funding for restoring. Other images present natural disasters that stroke momentarily, with a cinematic movement, inert, fossilized buildings. These unexpected happenings bring out an intrinsic dynamic of architecture that becomes apparent when architecture ceases to fulfil its habitational function. These natural, logistic or constructional

Fig. 2.4: Carlos Bunga, Annotated newspaper material, ©Carlos Bunga.

Fig. 2.5: Carlos Bunga, Metamorphosis, 2009, Miami Art Museum, ©Carlos Bunga and Elba Benitez Gallery.

Fig. 2.6: Carlos Bunga, Nomada III, 2008, Ink and collage on paper, ©Carlos Bunga.

'accidents', momentary come-backs from the chaos that precedes any built form, bring to the surface an unpredictable and ambiguous force of space that remains uncontrolled by the human. It also creates a micro-climate in which Bunga studies the laws that dominate the decomposition of form, as in a laboratory. His mere joining together of files – media-transmitted information and images – reveals how building is based on the devouring of matter and resources. He shows how consumption can dissolve or annul representation, and how a dominant social and political order has lost the means of critical self-analysis.

In another of Bunga's drawing series 'Nomada' (2008), android beings carry head-architecture. These hybrid walking buildings carry an architecture that has the configuration of a brain. Being mobile, they relocate the *memory* of lost spatial configuration. The figures could be seen as resulting from an ancestral digging after hypostases of coalescence between man and space. Rather than a type of dwelling where the human being lives *in* and is contained *by* architecture, these figures speak about memory and the possibility of architecture being memorized or individually archived as a patrimonial model carried by history and then *performed* by the individual. Nomad architecture shows how humans can store/archive architecture by *being it*, while layers of information are condensed and compressed into a new entity, 'mobile architecture', that carries all its data with it. In these drawings there is also a shift of focus from the objecthood of architecture to its environmental qualities.

Another means of attaining documentation that augments the presence and identity of architecture in Bunga's work is colour. It can appear as monochromatic paint layered on top of his cardboard installations (as in his work 'Metamorphosis', 2009) or in the form of pure pigment heaps that become construction materials ('Habitar Color', 2007). Pigment, as an essential dimension of colour, makes visible the idea of the spatiality of colour, whereas colour itself exhibits its interiority. Architecture coated in colour suggests a connection with the 'lived' dimension of time as a process of experiencing the transformations of architecture, when understood as an organic body. As matter transforms along various temporal cycles, colour experiences fluctuations in its intensity and quality. Repainting, or digging for hidden layers of colour, reveals temporal aspects that are released by matter, and, in this sense, colour functions as a document that constructs or reconstructs the transformations that architecture has gone through.

Fig. 2.7: Carlos Bunga, The Elba Benitez Project, 2005, Elba Benitez Gallery, Madrid, ©Carlos Bunga & Elba Benitez Gallery.

Ruin as documents

For Carlos Bunga 'ruin' is an essential term since it connotes the point where processes of construction and deconstruction (with which he constantly works) collide. Ruins are relevant as architectural presence, due to the dynamism and transformations in which their architectural form originates. In this sense, this notion explains approaches to the built form, encountered also in the works of other artists. Interesting also from a macro-urbanistic point of view is that they keep the record of construction and demolition measures in various historic phases. As a social presence, as a living vestige from past cultural epochs, the ruin contains an absence that makes up its identity more than its material residue. Through this temporal ellipse that a ruin contains, it is virtual and real at the same time. In this sense, documenting the transformation of architecture in time implies working with the void that it carries.

Beyond its visual form, a ruin transports an indiscernible embodied potentiality in time. Since it comprises juxtaposed moments, it represents a form of organization which is organically connected with other spaces. It carries not only past forms of the same construction, but also contaminations from other environments, different cross-connections with distant spaces, with which the initial building has been related in different circumstances. The decay of matter with its physical outcome happens in a natural way without human intervention. In this way the ruin reproduces a non-human temporality, which remains inaccessible to man. Ruins are virtual yet material spaces that represent not only the past, but also the future, through their form in the present. Through the progressive destruction of its form, a ruin creates room for new spatial configurations and therefore belongs to the future. It is also an architectonic form, which, in stepping out of its stability, becomes dynamic. Its decay is a temporal process through which its form adapts constantly to a temporal rhythm. On the other hand, the processuality of time achieves a material, visible form in a ruin. The ruin, as a form of re-contextualization, lets different spatial and temporal configurations confront each other. It also serves the function of disrupting an established hierarchy and provoking a redistribution of value in space.

The gallerist Michael Krome (2009 interview) talks about the cultural memory, which every object carries and which is especially forceful in Bunga's work. Krome calls this the memorability of the construction which transports with it its own decay. Bunga's ephemeral intervention in a specific historic urban context with its heavy load of time, creates what Krome calls 'both a concrete and abstract space at the same time'. In his comments on Bunga's work, Krome mentions the 2009 destruction by implosion of the state archive in Köln/(Cologne) and the capacity of Bunga's work to deliver a commentary and to have an impact and an agency with regard to this recent event. Seen from this point of view, every work produced and immersed in a certain context is naturally responsive to other events that happen concomitantly, but most of all it is *responsible* for its cultural actuality.

This interplay of concrete intervention and simulation is reinforced through Bunga's preferred material involved in almost all his works: cardboard. Cardboard itself functions like a document of time. Its particularity relates to the fact that it is connected to a permanent present: it is ephemeral but is the result of a line of infinite recycling, an accumulation of material in time. Cardboard reveals a contemporary attitude to materiality based on re-utilization, transformation and adaptation, but is also perennial since it endures through transformation, carrying its own history with it. It decomposes and can be recycled as a new piece of cardboard that is always equal to a previous one and it inspires a flexible approach to architecture. It is simulating a more durable material, which it can replace only for a limited amount of time (since it degrades very fast), but at the same time it is strong, supporting a heavy load.

In an article on the idea of ruins in European culture, Rosa Olivares (Olivares 2008) describes the ruins in contemporary society as a product between various different cosmeticized and artificially aesthetized products. These well-packed ruins make it possible for the consumer to assimilate tragedy and catastrophe, of which ruins are concrete consequences. In the European tradition, ruins are, for the elite, an aesthetic category. Rosa Olivares questions the circumstances in which ruins became symbols with positive connotations in European history, particularly since the Renaissance, symbols of noble values, transformation, progress and aesthetical intensity. She sees the contemporary ruin as exposed to a very rapid transformation from its moment of destruction to its transformation into an artistic product. Contrary to the ruin in past epochs, which was romanticized due to lack of information about the social aspects of the catastrophes from which it resulted, nowadays the aesthetization of the ruin is a result of ignoring the human aspects of the catastrophe, which only in this artificially cleaned shape can be transformed into an artistic product. Unlike the ruins of the past, which gain a mythical character through the power of collective memory, we share the same temporal sequence with the ruins of our society. These ruins of the present cannot have a romantic charge and cannot be a symbol of reconstruction, but can only be a symbol of deconstruction. For Rosa Olivares the preoccupation of contemporary art with ruins is an experiment that comes from agony – the agony to have to accept an unacceptable reality, which can be regarded only in an objectified way.

The quality of a ruin to recall memories as well as collective symbols has been used to map urban space with symbolic content, as carried out for example in the re-functionalization of industrial ruins, in the refurbishing of abandoned urban sites and so on. The ambiguity of ruins as commodified objects of cultural consumption that embody simultaneously a lived history that is incommunicable is captured by Tim Edensor in his term 'memoryscapes' (2005: 133). A 'ruin scape' can be used to imprint memory in space by the means of remembrance effects, often ignoring the historic reality that the present brings – with the objective of raising the marketability of these ruined architectures.

In recent artistic initiatives these critical aspects have been included in the body of the work. In the works discussed here, the fragmented architectural form is not associated to various movements of revival, nostalgia and historicism. It seems rather to be close to the understanding of the architectural fragment in modernity, where it surpassed its wistful and melancholic load from previous eras, and became a sign of shock and estrangement in art and film. At this time form and the iconographic symbols with which it was historically associated were dissociated.

The combative fragment of modernity, incomplete and broken, was a result of production and consumption and, at the same time, a result of resistance against them. In 'Warped Space', Antony Vidler (2000) comments that the postmodern fragment, 'the quote', signifies a regression to a romantic vision of history. An ironic composition, it guarantees the comfort and tradition of history, with its mission to absorb the unease of modernity (Vidler 2000: 150). Surpassing this dual interpretation of the fragment from the perspective of modernity versus postmodernity, the use of the fragment in the works treated here can be delineated by Vidler's idea of the 'shifted fragment', a piece detached from the whole and that has no symbolic load. It has no allegorical value and opposes a linear, historical temporality; it can be understood as estranged from its initial context.

Fig. 2.8: Carlos Bunga ,Volumen no articulado, 2010, Cardboard, paint and wood on Carrara marble pedestal, Sculpture at Postmonument: XIV Carrara International Biennale of Sculpture, Carrara, Italia, ©Carlos Bunga.

Fig. 2.9: Carlos Bunga, House Plan, 2010, Cardboard, paint and wood on Carrara marble pedestal", Sculpture at Postmonument: XIV Carrara International Biennale of Sculpture, Carrara, Italia, ©Carlos Bunga.

Archive and monuments

Ruins are a living archive. In his work, Bunga addresses the fact that the process of archiving alters the nature of reality, while at the same time insisting on the deep connection between archiving and destruction, and observing how annihilation of memory determines the drive to archive. In the 2007–2008 video 'More Spaces for Other Constructions' he rubs out reproductions of well-known buildings, ones that already belong to a common 'Archive'. This process Bunga calls 'painting *with* space'. Throughout Bunga's work destruction is deeply anarchic, not only by deleting an archival order and opening it up to new criteria, but also by showing that to achieve democratization it is essential to allow access and direct participation in the archive, to facilitate open intervention in the constitution of an archive.

Bunga works precisely with a dimension of the archiving, that is not simply recording the past, but also *forming* it. The past is actually shaped by the future, which retrospectively or retroactively endows it with meaning. Derrida relates participation to time in *Archive Fever*. He explains that the technological power of the archive determines the nature of what is archived and as the content and the meaning of the archive is reshaped by all the people that participate in it, the archive is dependent on what is coming, 'on what will have come' (Derrida 1998b: 46). Its openness towards what might come in the future determines that it is impossible for the archive to be saturated or closed. This future-oriented dimension of the archive is that which creates, as Derrida stresses, its possibility to be always reinterpreted, and also our political and ethical responsibility towards it.

The constructions encountered throughout this volume can be considered as *negative monuments*, characterized by fragility and non-functionality. They are distinguished on one hand by monumental proportions (independent of their sizes), but on the other hand they quote familiar objects in daily or domestic use. Carlos Bunga's sculptures with unspecified titles like 'House Plan' (2010), 'Untitled' (2002), 'Unarticulated Volume' (2010), etc., shown for example in his exhibition 'Unmonumental' 2007 in the New Museum, or in the XIV International Carrara Biennial, 2010, present ambiguous formations. They are rich in art-historical references, alluding to the secular heritage of Carrara marble, used during Italian art from the Renaissance to the present. A paradigmatic architectural morphology (including columns, house plans, an amphitheatre or towers) made of ephemeral cardboard is mounted on precious marble pedestals. Bunga's works is always saturated with art-historical citations, but at the same time these unmask what they are quoting. In his 2009 'Ruins Projects' or in the 'Mutations' series, the monuments are half-decayed, fictive, bricollaged and non-colossal, and finally they defy existing historical narratives. Anti-hegemonical, since they do not belong to or symbolically mark a certain territory, they affirm a conception of the monument in reverse.

The relationship between the monument and the document has been extensively written about, and in Bunga's architecturally-oriented work, this connection comes constantly to the surface. Derrida mentions in 'Archive Fever' that the monument is deeply related to *amnesia* and *hypomnema* – the fading of memory (Derrida 1998a: 11). At the same time, 'The archivization produces as much as it records the event' (Derrida 1998a: 17). The monument is therefore built from destruction and forgetfulness and, as an archive, it works against itself. In this sense Bunga's monuments are as much political experiences, as they are ahistorical. They refer to an unrepresentable reality that is not capable of being experienced in real time. Another interpretation of the archive, which is relevant for the approach to historic time and to processes of documentation expressed in these works, is that of Paul Ricoeur. He shows (Ricoeur 2006: 67) a gap between the present meaning attributed to documents and the original meaning of 'having the function to teach'. Instead, archives now have the function of acting as evidence, to constitute a proof. Any random trace left by history can therefore now be interpreted as a document, and Ricoeur talks about these traces as 'involuntary testimonies'. Citing Jacques Le Goff, Ricoeur (Ricoeur 2006: 67) reminds us that archives were called '*monuments*' until the middle of the 19th century. It is in this line of thought that monuments are now connected to a predetermined final goal: to commemorate.

In recent works that deal with historic patrimony and memory, there is a defined tendency to construct non-selective archives in which not only exemplary facts are chosen to have a representative function, but also minor incidents and quotidian experiences are considered relevant for a historic time span. Carlos Bunga's collection of sculptures with Carrara pedestals, for example, are composite monuments, since they entail fragments from various temporal cycles, material reminiscences that *involuntarily* commemorate art history. He implants them into his work in a way that deprives them of any symbolic content, serving no particular discourse. In this way these historic fragments gain a new objectivity, and can assert a critical position in their new habitat.

In the interview on pages 69–71 it becomes clear how Sancho Silva deals with the monumental character of architecture as a deposit of value. In the 2007 interview, Silva talks about the political dimension of public space, of how design structures social relations and about his way of destabilizing and distorting space, which is for him *a medium*. Silva calls space a 'shifter', a grammatical term that can act at the same time in various contexts and that can determine the changeover of a certain grammatical conjuncture. 'I am interested in abstracting the potential of the space in terms of architecture' (Silva 2007 interview). In Sancho Silva's 'Orange Works' series, started in 2004 and developed with John Hawks in Brooklyn, New York,

Fig. 2.10: Carlos Bunga, Untitled, 2002, Cardboard, packing tape and paint, ©Carlos Bunga.

Fig. 2.11: Carlos Bunga, Nomada III, 2008, Ink and collage on paper, ©Carlos Bunga.

basic constructions with ambiguous shapes, without any label, are placed in public space and are adopted for use by citizens according to their momentary needs. The basic, familiar and universal architectural shapes, not yet completely rooted in the context, were easily re-adapted, turned into bus stations, benches or abodes for the homeless.

Seen as temporary monuments, they offer an alternative to the commodification of communitarian space through the formation of a collective nostalgia for the past and some established architectural forms and make an architectural proposal for a flexible conservation of historic patrimony that is attentive to the present and is capable of re-functionalization.

In Yukihiro Taguchi's works 'Moment' and 'Auf' (2006), mentioned for example in the interview on page 69, a history is externalized that annuls, or rather reverses, the values which it exhibits. In 'Auf' (2006) Taguchi lifted a gallery carpet up and the visitor could step into the space under the carpet, where the exhibition actually took place. This new space brings into question the legitimacy and status of the institutional space. The work mistrusts the inherited and seldom questioned social and professional conventions that institutional space accommodates. •

Interviews

Interview with Yukihiro Taguchi, May 2007

Q: Tension is a principle according to which you built your installations. Tension does point to the instability of space. In which way does this principle sustain architecture and in which way is such an architecture 'usable'?

Y.T.: One of my first preoccupations with space was tension, tension between objects in space. I have made in Tokyo performances and installations like 'Tension' and 'Supportable Space', both in 2003, where I have suspended in a room various objects only by the existing tension between them as a sustaining force. In these works danger also has an essential role that makes the experience more acute and brings into consciousness these forces. Any slightest change of the position of a single object in this installation would cause the whole construction to fall apart. The visitors felt this tension while entering the space and they were afraid of its effects.

Fig. 2.12: Yukihiro Taguchi, Giftset, 2007, ©Yukihiro Taguchi.

What interests me are the relations in space that result between any objects. In the presence of two objects we become aware of space. In my works with air bags I am marking the space/the air between two objects, with the plastic bag that encompasses it. There are spaces that remain usually not noticed; we are not aware of their existence. I am not alone in a certain space since, without me, the other objects cannot exist. The simple fact of me staying here means that the earth exists, and these are the situations that I try to find through my works. I think it is important not to lose these insights. In relation to this I am using titles with double meanings that show this duality, as in, for example, 'Gift' (2006). The excess of air is poison – the word '*Gift*' in German, but air is also a 'gift', in English. I have also included people in these experiments in my work with air bags, and let them play different games inside the balloon as the air is slowly coming out. You can watch from the outside their movements getting slowed down. As it becomes warm inside, their movements change their expressivity, become unnatural, while the audience outside perceives it like a moving sculpture. If I have only chairs inside the air bags, these begin to move, due to the progressive lack of air, and it seems the chairs alone start to make a performance. In the same way I have played with the word '*allein*', alone in German. All+*EIN* is a very interesting word. 'All' in English and '*ein*', one in German, signify for me the connection between me as an individual and the relations that I have with everything around me. Only through these relations can I exist alone.

I was thinking in a similar way while making the works 'Moment' (2007), and 'Auf' (2006), where I lifted the floor of the gallery space to release a new space beneath. The titles are also relevant here. Moment is an instant from a movement, and usually we cannot notice its micro-changes. When I removed the wooden floor panels in the gallery, new moments were released or emerged: the moments of particular situations that consumed in that space, moments buried in the surface, and moments from the time of all those who participated in this action. When I put the wood panels back with Daniel Lima, the gallerist, we thought that the space had experienced a break in its spatial continuity, and asked ourselves where these moments had all gone. I do not wish to add anything or remove something from the space as I find it, but I intend to reverse the situation in order to catch possible moments of the relations in space. It is a reverse of self-evidence in order to understand it.

Interview with Sancho Silva, August 2007

Q: In which way do you construct space according to a principle dictated by vision?

S.S.:   Vision is one way to create space. Space in general structures perception, like a house, for example, which is structuring your vision, through doors and windows, from the inside to the outside. Vision is also an important element in the construction of space. This is not the only one, because there is also movement. I use movement by giving different possibilities of movement to the person who inhabits a space: corridors, different routes to go from point A to point B, blocking different passages and opening others. Architecture conditions movement, it gives in itself instructions, it directs and it determines how you perform different movements. I am interested in abstracting the potential of the space in terms of architecture. Usually you live in these environments and you are not aware so much how it affects you, how it shapes what you see, how you move. I try to create a force which stabilizes this potential. That is why I do constructions that deny the function of space, so you become aware of these mechanisms of manipulation. I always try to have two points of view in the works. One point of view in which you are immersed in a mechanism, and you cannot orient yourself in it, and you cannot understand it since you are controlled by it. Then I try to construct a second point of view within the same work, where you see the mechanism from outside, you understand how it works and you can then dismantle the mechanism in your mind.

Q: Can you talk about your idea of 'shortcut' in relation to space? One of your works has this title, but this seems to be also a working method for you? You cut architecture after principles that reveal to perception its condensed structure. 'Shortcut', in your work, is on the one hand a constructional solution, and on the other it describes a mental process that your works generate in relation to the understanding of space.

S.S.:   In the work 'Shortcut' (2002), I have constructed a *functional* shortcut through a house: a short way to reach from one street to the next street, through the building. You don't have to go around the house to get to the other street, but you can cut through the house. 'Shortcut' is a distortion; it is something that has been twisted. You have the normal trajectory, but this is a faster or different way of getting there, which takes you away from the normal trajectory.

It is mental in the sense that this process can be experienced. It is this duality: physical is also mental. It is like a pane of glass, which is very thick and through it you see distorted. If reality hadn't been distorted through the glass, you wouldn't be able to see the glass. Distortion makes the process and the medium/the mechanism visible, so this is mental and physical as well.

The first moment that one experiences my works there is something that attracts the visitor, but also something that creates confusion. One loses orientation since I propose an enigma, and the public is invited to solve the puzzle. This mental process is embodied in the movement of the person who is experiencing it. The work is to be used, it is not only visual, and I base my work on this duality as a dialectical experience.

Q: In your work, architecture is used as a tool for transmitting information about a specific environment, and it is also delimiting a certain social or cultural environment that it comments upon. In 'Mus-papilionoidea' (2001), in 'Faro' (2008), 'Vertizon' (2004), or 'Cyclopean Eye Berlin' (2006), your machines of vision surpass the obvious limits of architecture that occupies a territory and extend its agency beyond the actual construction.

S.S.:   Architecture is a media. The medium of cinema and the medium of a house alike transform perception while making a selection from reality, and architecture is in this sense a technology. Like any other media, architecture shows how perception is constructed, how it can be manipulated, and how it can be developed and changed. Perception starts from the body and from its way of reacting to technology, it's the same with architecture. Language is also a way to construct/affect perception. An image with a sentence, for example, changes completely the image. But also language changes the image through the way you refer to an image. This is the way technology and media are appearing in my work. In fact architecture is very strongly related to the eye and vice versa, because architecture is a machine of vision, of perception. The way it blocks, the way it opens, the way it frames, the way it hides, the way it reveals are very similar to the way the eye is working.

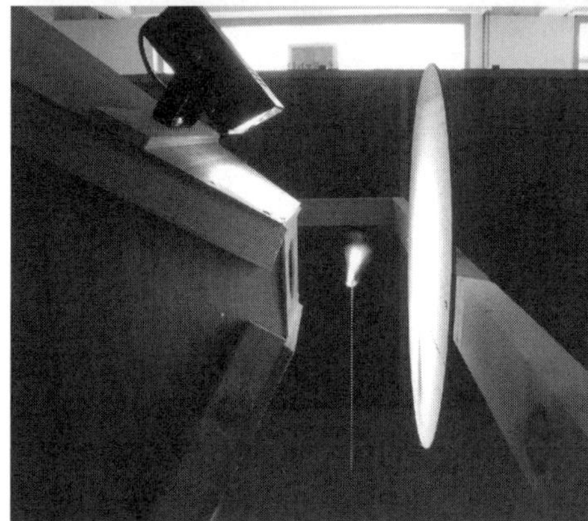

Fig. 2.13-2.14: Sancho Silva, Dolle Mol, 2008, Antwerp, Photo, ©Kristien Daem, ©Sancho Silva.

Fig. 2.15: Sancho Silva, Dolle Mol, 2008, Antwerp, Photo, ©Kristien Daem, ©Sancho Silva.

In my public-space works with John Hawks, the 'Orange Works' (an ongoing project since 2004, in New York), we have involved materials that are used to limit the use of public space. By doing this ourselves, we assume an authority that is in fact now ours and we occupy public spaces with our constructions, without permission. In this process we can then see the degree of resistance that the place has, by observing how people react to a new spatial situation. In 'Bus Stop', we have constructed a shelter for a bus stop that was in use, and applied the orange material used in construction works, and people started to use it. By using it they naturalized it, and the ambiguous construction became a bus stop. Once, when we were on the bus, we asked the bus driver: 'what is this construction?' and he said: 'It is a bus stop!', like it was the most natural thing. When things get functional, they then acquire a certain authority and they last longer. This can be a strategy to occupy a space: to create a function.

In another 'Orange Work': 'Open House/Rest House' (2006), we constructed a small house, which people started using because it was an empty place in Brooklyn, and people would sit there to eat or rest. We put up signs to get the attention of the passers-by, and also erected white walls on which we were sticking images from our project and other projects from the area, encouraging people to respond in the form of graffiti or text to the information. People assumed that the construction was from the electricity company, the electricity company thought it was from the gas company, and in this ambiguity each created a place for himself. The police finally became very anxious about the pavilion and destroyed it, and people took the wood from the structure to use it for other purposes.

We also intended these works to be a way to test the relationship between public and private space and the thin lines between them that are sometimes physically, sometimes mentally, constructed. The intention was to create works that are on the borderline between the private and the public. My strategy is making what you expect to be public seem private, and what you expect to be private to be of public use. No place is vacant, lacking authority or appropriation, so no space can be completely public or totally private, but I am interested in our expectations of them and how this actually works. Often there is a big gap between how it works in reality and how we think it works. There is also a political dimension here, of course. How is the city designed? How it is meant to be structuring social relations?

Interview with Michael Krome, July 2009[4]

Q: Would you like to talk about the relationship that Carlos Bunga established with the architecture of the gallery building, with the architectural statement that your gallery transmits, and with the entire environment of Marxist urbanism in which the gallery is placed[5]?

M.K.: In the discussions with Bunga about the gallery space, we have talked about the impact of his work, which opens up the gallery space, but at the same time brings a melancholic, agile and poetical input, which it exerts upon the initial space. His very basic architectonic vocabulary, cardboard and tape bring a fragility, but at the same time a memorability to this socialistic representational architecture. His work creates a dialectic between the urban space of the gallery and the exterior space in which it is located. A coincidence was the implosion of the state archive in Köln/Cologne at the time of our exhibition, which made us talk contextually about the space of the exhibition. The implosion carried big symbolic power: urban memory had collapsed, houses were falling down, exterior walls remained without support and reminded us of Bunga's painted surfaces, which seem to be traces of abstract spatial divisions, which carry allusions to interior space and used space. In the *remnants* of the building in Cologne you could see a blue-painted inner wall, the part of a door with a towel hanging and completely destroyed façades. If you look at Bunga's photographic work, these analogies becomes obvious. The remains of the explosion and Bunga's installations both reveal an abstracted interior space, they reveal *forgotten histories* and *lost spaces*, as the rhythmical, socialistic shapes carry the remains of the typology of Karl Friedrich Schinkel's (1781–1841) architecture.

From a sociological point of view, I consider the Karl-Marx-Allee to be not very oriented towards the human. The architecture permits few traces of human life: you can see very few people; the proportions of the windows are small, oriented towards the interior, as opposed to the usual Berlin neighbourhood, where life is going on in the streets. With minimal, logistical, trash materials, which are at the same time very fragile, Bunga builds an architecture which is ephemeral, but at the same time breaks with sedimented formulas of architecture. The fact that the history of cardboard is connected to a progressive industrialization and the development of an industry – of packaging – is also especially interesting in this context. Bunga's architecture has also something infantile about it, in the sense of being childish and extremely creative: he is always constructing 'his own thing!' It is a very personal work when you know its history: Bunga searched obsessively for abstract painting appearing naturally in public space. On the one hand he exhibited his own painting in outdoor space, and performed a displacement process. On the other hand, by finding natural abstract painting in outdoor space, he posed the question: 'Do I still have to paint?'

Bunga's work also carries very strong allusions to Potemkin architecture and this is also another critical potential of it. It raises another important question for urbanism, namely how does a human being open up to public space, how does man live, how does he encapsulate himself in satellite towns? My question has always been how can art discuss public space as a space of thought, how can art improve it, optimize it and differentiate it?

Q: You have mentioned the melancholy of Bunga's work; what do you consider to be at the heart of this?

M.K.:   His works for me are melancholic due to their chromatic effect, the washed off colours and the associations that they recall. The paint has an old-style effect; the colours carry in them another time […] His work is melancholic also as a replica of façade-architecture, which is hermetical. Bunga brings an opening that introduces the human proportions. And although his installations are not narrative, they create routes in these spaces inside spaces. Maybe this is too personal, but I perceive the monochromes he uses as Cuban tristesse-colours, that evoke a better time, but which are in a state of decay already. Colour is itself a texture, and the romanticism that lies in the choice of colour, connected to the use of cardboard, which is itself perishable and flaking off, comes mainly from the temporalization of colour – a colour that is not necessarily well-applied.

Q: Do you consider this a critical statement? There is always an allusion to the institution within which he is creating his work.

M.K.:   Yes, we could consider his attitude in relation to my gallery space also as being very cynical: the Stasi socialist monument in which the gallery is situated is in fact a late fascistic achievement, a coercive architecture. And in the middle of it stands the person Carlos Bunga, a modern man, who is a contemporary mixture of anthropological designs and descents, a foreign body.

Socialist architecture destroyed the *Wilhelminian*[6] and interweaved it with the cheapest materials. The architecture of Bunga, himself a foreign body, formulates a response in the sense of him using these unrepresentative materials and building on an existing structure that has been a product of many other superimposed historical layers. After the show he flies away and what remains of his work is a pile of cardboard. For me it has been always difficult to know until where his criticality goes. He is himself not a cynical person.

Q: Do you mean that his criticality is originating in his particular approach to architecture rather than in a direct statement?

M.K.:   Yes, exactly.

Q: Where did you meet him?

M.K.:   At 'Art Basel', in 2008. There he had a similar critical impulse. 'Art Unlimited' is an appendage to Art Basel, which was created to give more space to the artists and to involve the audience, the artists and the curators, who were already tired of the art fair system. The exclusion of different artistic formats from the fair, led to the decision to organize 'Art Unlimited', where big format works could be shown. Bunga defied, once again, expectations regarding his work 'Ruins' (2008) and showed here the foundations of a work, remains that carried a very melancholic atmosphere. It seemed to me an affront towards the predominant attitude that stressed the possibilities of building something big, of showing everything. From a critical point of view his work was a very good choice and represented his statement to the format of 'Art Basel'.

Q: Considering the flexibility of Bunga's work in adapting to different contexts of meaning, do you find it necessary to relate the term 'performativity' to his work?

M.K.: I see performativity as connected with the use of his work, or rather with its aesthetic agency. Use is an extreme form of agency and its aesthetic. In Bunga's work the interactivity between the observer and the work is conceived in ambiguous terms: the viewer does not have a clear role. What Bunga's work requires from the audience is a capacity to react introspectively. There are still many people who have an apparently avant-garde conception of art, and for whom the material and the perfection of form are criteria for appreciation. This position sees art deriving from proficiency. In Bunga's case the idea needs the destruction of perfection. In this I also see the radicality of Bunga's work. There have also been many misunderstandings attributing a ghetto association with his work, which are in my opinion not relevant and not positive for his work.

   With regard to the lived history of the architectural monument in which my gallery is located, Bunga's work makes a clear statement. It has also been said that Karl-Marx-Allee is the last undeveloped boulevard in Europe, in the sense that it is not made for people strolling, being together and parking their cars; it is not made for living. It is not a boulevard in a practical sense and I hope that art as a medium can balance this lack of social communication. What interests me in this gallery is not the neutral space, the white cube, but rather its *demanding context*. Bunga brings here a hope: it is a melancholic hope, maybe punk-rock, strong and weak at the same time. And what we wish to do in this gallery is contextual and not always forced, not always didactic […].

Interview with Cristian Rusu, April 2010

Q: Being a scenographer and artist, how do you approach architecture with scenographic devices? Do you regard architecture as a 'setting' for your ideas? In what way do the two approaches inform each other?

C.R.: As a scenographer I have an intimate connection with space, and a lot of the preoccupations that I have in the theatre are reflected somehow within my artistic practice. As an artist I first approach the public space as a critical, ideological space. I worked with Mihai Pop from the group 'Duo van der Mixt' at the time of the extreme nationalist local administration in our home town of Cluj, Romania, which lasted from 1992 to 2004. In 1997, all the public space in the city was polluted with nationalist ideology. At that time, we carried out fieldwork based on virtual interventions, which we staged ourselves in specific public areas of Cluj that were deformed by ideology, in order to exorcise the ugliness of those sites. We also gathered thousands of photos depicting those public space anomalies. And we did it with an extremely critical eye!

Fig. 2.16: Cristian Rusu, Pavillon Tyrol, 2007–2008, Exhibition view, European Travellers, Mücsarnok Budapest 2012, Photo, ©Cristian Rusu ©Cristian Rusu & Galeria Plan B.

Fig. 2.17: Cristian Rusu, Untitled, 2007, photography, Photo, ©Alexandra Croitoru, ©Cristian Rusu & Galeria Plan B.

During one residency at Künstlerhaus Büchsenhausen in Austria in 2007, I started to work on what I used to call *spatial clichés*. My first project was connected to sound and image, when a projection of a light spectre on a building in Innsbruck was coordinated with recorded sounds that connected with the image.

The final work that I created there was 'Pavillon Tyrol' (2007), a Greek temple-shaped pavilion that has a mountain instead of a roof, that recalls the environment where the art work was conceived. In addition, it also delivers a critical commentary on the aesthetic and ideological manipulation of Alpine imagery that became a cliché of the monumental geometry of power of past totalitarian systems. This work generated an entire 'Alpine Serie' on which I am now working.

I am also interested in the Russian avant-garde, in constructivism which is intimately connected to ideology. I am fascinated by their spatial projects in 2D or 3D: El Lissitzky, for instance, with his 'PROUN Spaces' created in two or three dimensions, or Rodchenko's and Malevich's spatial constructions, or Kurt Schwitter's 'Merzbau' installation (which filled his entire environment). For me, they belong to the arena of visions of utopia. We are always connected to space and everything becomes tri-dimensional. Yesterday in Berlin I saw an advertisement for a movie, which said: 'The Fight of the Titans Starts in 3D!' and under it a line: 'But it also can be seen in 2D'. An alternative was given! This is a mutation in the visual perception of space!

Q: Does the recreation of recognizable architectural paradigms or your suggestion of a symbolic architecture carry a specific polemic in your work?

C.R.: During my residency in Innsbruck I became more and more fascinated by the aesthetic category of the sublime (as Kant and Burke described it in the 18th century), which implies monumentality, mystery, fear, force, melancholy, and an imaginary unknown territory that implies also a metaphysical dimension of contemplation. I am now working on transposing this dimension into the visual, concentrating on pure emotion, and I am getting visibly further away from a critical perspective.

I have now developed a fascination for the Romantics and therefore my work 'Untitled' (a photograph from 2007), which is a deliberate reference of the famous Caspar David Friedrich's 'Wanderer above the Sea of Fog'. That is a state of mind, not simply an image! I wanted to exercise our contemporary eye on the domain of the sublime, by placing ourselves in the painting, in that space. In my particular case, that image was made twice as intense in my experience of intense emotion […].

In my visual research with photography, I have tried to understand a type of light, an effect, the almost theatrical scenography of nature, and I came to understand that nature is as it is, and that it is us that cut off from it in a deliberate act of conferring significance. One example is my 'Untitled' series of four photographs (2008), or – a more radical one – the image with fog 'Fog' (2008), that problematized volume and depth through light.

Q: I was asking myself if it was digitally manipulated?

C.R.:   No, I do not manipulate photography, but I also do not consider myself a photographer. I do not investigate the whole visual reality that surrounds me through photography. I do not manipulate photography, and I prefer to take hundreds of photos in order to find the right one.

Q: Why?

C.R.:   I believe in the unique moment. I make an examination through a series of images, but then I exhibit only one of them. I normally never shoot with flash, but here, for example, in 'Fog', the flash triggered automatically, and I realized that the white spots that got recorded represented the materiality of the fog that otherwise is not visible.

Q: Are you interested in the idea of the model in itself, or do these models function as a representation of the final installation, as a memory of it?

C.R.:   I am concerned about both: the *idea* of pavilion, but also its transposition, that is, its memory, because the idea will then multiply; it does not have a fixed formula. I am, for example, interested in the relationship between architecture and natural shapes (like the mountain), and as soon as I have put an idea in motion, I have to find concrete solutions for its transposition. I like working in consistent materials, like concrete, for example. I first created 'Pavillon Tyrol' in perishable materials used in scenography (like wood, expanded polystyrene, cloth, papier-mâché etc.), but this was generally only because of an insufficient budget. I work often in these materials to create the models, but then I try to transpose them into solid materials. This is also the domain of utopia that we were talking about, because most of my works are just models, waiting to be transposed somehow into full-scale pieces, somewhere in public space […].

Q: Tell me about how you turn movement into space in your video 'Calle della Morte'[7] (2008), where, while keeping a fixed frame on the name of the street in Venice, your hands start to tremble until you lose the image. How do you induce tri-dimensionality, and life with spiritual connotations, into a bi-dimensional image?

C.R.:   The text (the name of the street) for me in this image looks like a constructivist black-and-white graphic collage. Although the image is minimal and bi-dimensional, what I wanted to attain is a sort of performative video on the instability of space. But the important idea for me here was the disequilibrium of space, which I also work on in other pieces. The entire exhibition in Berlin in Plan B Gallery ('Space Itself', 2009) was actually based on a total spatial disequilibrium. In the drawings I made an architectural pattern, that I then shifted slightly, which again transmitted movement into the architecture, which I then transposed into the tri-dimensional architecture of the gallery space, with direct charcoal drawings in one niche of the gallery space. In these drawings we depart from a bi-dimensional space of drawing and through this shift, we get

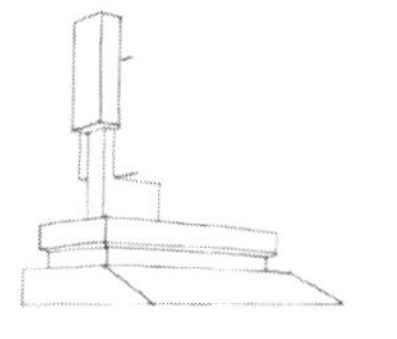

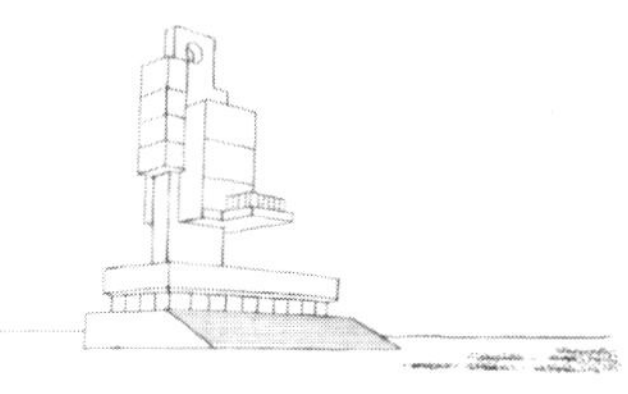

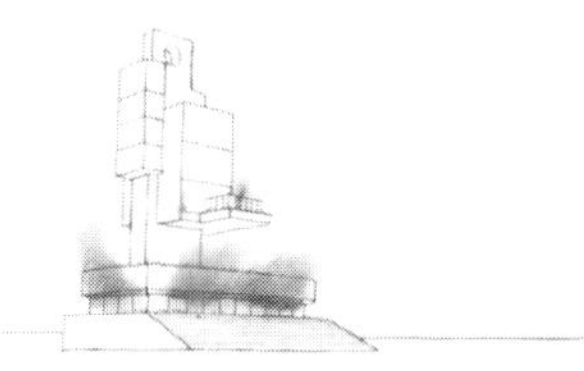

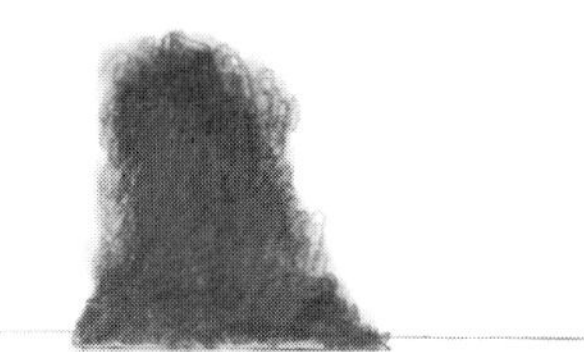

Fig. 2.18: Cristian Rusu, 45" Revolution, 2009, Video-animation, 45", Photo, ©Cristian Rusu.

into a tri-dimensional space, based solely on the disequilibrium of the stability of space that a simple line induces.

The video 'Untitled' (2008), with the pages of a book moving, also comes from the domain of purist minimalism, but is more poetical.

Q: You actually create a de-phasing between time and space. Space traverses one rhythm, while time takes another route. Their conjunction is displacing, shifting these rhythms. Are you interested in these disjunctions, or do you approach them from another perspective?

C.R.: In the case of the book video it was an accident that I appreciated. I was reading and my breath moved the pages. There was a kind of invisible energy that connected me with the book. That energy was finally visible! Usually I work from a momentary observation, which afterwards transforms into what it should be.

In '45 Seconds Revolution', a video-animation on utopia and constructivism, I tried to create an architectonical space that cannot stand up. I made it in monstrous proportion, with constructivist aesthetic criteria. In 45 seconds it is built and destroyed by people, while they also die, together with the building. It is a micro-revolution, a commentary on totalitarian utopias and everything they can generate. These aspects are for me both monstrous and fascinating at the same time. I read a commentary of one of the leaders of the Party at the time of Stalin, which said: 'We have to consider that not even the present position of the mountains, the waters and the plains is definitive'. In my video-animation, the monument is created and destroyed by its builders, since it cannot exist physically, although it is based on constructional visionary ideas.

One of my next projects is to draw in lead. I have taken some pipes, cut them up, and made lead pencils, thinking of Dürer, who was drawing with silver pencils. Lead has a very special grey tone, and a metal glow, which gives it a special preciousness. Also you cannot erase it, which is a big challenge for me. Doing a drawing that cannot be deleted afterwards has to do with a sort of performance for me.

Q: Which is the critical potential of utopia, the way you can work critically with it?

C.R: The aesthetic category of the sublime and also utopia's sublime are connected to a zone of lack of control. The fascination for it stems from here, like the fascination for death, as a domain of the unknown. I am not working with the critique of a certain event, but with this domain. I wish to make critical work with very simple, almost purist means.

Q: What is the role of the human in your work? The human is rarely represented visually in your work.

C.R: In my work, the point of view is always mine, it is very personal, whether I make an abstract or a figurative work (meaning if the human figure appears, or not). It will always be me that directs the point of view, according to the energy that emanates from the objects, according to the subject and the medium. I think it is important to understand the medium with which you work, or, what works with the medium you choose, even though it sounds trivial. There are many excellent ideas transposed using an unfortunate choice of medium, or excellent media used with very small ideas. So I choose very carefully the right medium for my works. Yet there is always a human eye behind all that. That romantic, melancholic gaze which I try to share […].

NOTES

1   These terms were established by Derrida himself.
2   The architects represented in the exhibition were: Zaha Hadid, Bernard Tschumi, Rem Koolhaas, Coop Himmelblau, Daniel Libeskind, Peter Eisenman, Frank O. Gehry.
3   Logocentrism is a philosophical term that regards the written or spoken word as superior to other forms of expression. The 'logos' is seen as most accurately representing a superior essence/truth.
4   Carlos Bunga's exhibition 'Marxitecture' in the Krome gallery took place in 2009. The interview with Michael Krome, the gallery's owner, took place a short time after the show.
5   The Karl-Marx-Allee, on which the Micheal Krome gallery is situated, is a monumental socialist boulevard built in the German Democratic Republic between 1952 and 1960 in Berlin Friedrichshain.
6   The architecture developed in the time of Wilhelm II mainly in Austria, Germany and in the colony Namibia was an adaptation of neo-baroque elements, meant to express the aspirations of imperial power of the Kaiser.
7   The name of the street in Venice means 'Street of Death'.

CHAPTER 3
Leap into documentation: The post-conceptual space

Overall argument

Performativity and the deconstruction of the object have turned, in the previous chapters, to be agencies by which the virtual can be experienced in post-digital experiences and environments. In this chapter, the images, theoretical insights and interviews will reveal how documenting past or virtual forms of buildings is a means of deconstructing them and bringing them into motion. Through documentation, past actualized or unactualized forms that architecture, an environment or a situation carry with them can become visible and take a concrete shape. It is this performative, mutated object that makes the experience of the virtual possible to the viewer.

The digital world is populated by objects which tend to be perfect, complete and which are illusionistic. On the contrary, in the works described here, objects and environments carry the mark of human intervention and exhibit the effect of the often unpredictable social or political context inscribed upon them. Temporal and spatial incongruencies that are part of these trajectories, can be therefore seen as contesting the vision of digital progress, coherence and sublimation.

In this chapter the role of conceptualism and post-conceptualism comes to attention regarding the specific construction of what could be called a post-digital object. I have identified a certain direction in conceptual art that sets a high value on the material qualities of objects, partially by the means of documentation. I consider that this particular interest in the potential and agency of matter is essential in the formulation of conceptualism and has been transmitted into late post-conceptual art, where a return to the object takes place, transgressing the limits of the so-called 'hard' conceptualism. By invoking recent works, I would like to propose that this post-conceptual approach has also played a substantial role in the overlap between the virtual and the real.

Involving documentation in the body of the work is a defining trait of conceptual art. Documentation was employed in the works described here and in similar installations as a means to respond to the context, but also to break the continuity of the objects. Voided environments emerged that 'documented' past events. Further down, these will be linked to a long tradition of iconophobia and destroying artistic image. Conceptual Art of the 1960s and 1970s almost caused the material component of the work to disappear. Artists such as Joseph Kosuth contributed to the self-annulment of artwork, determined by a theoretical dissolution of the object of art, which sought to renounce artwork as visible form altogether, by replacing physical work with pure idea, with philosophy. With this conceptual dissolution, minimalism achieved a formal reduction of the object of art.

Certain approaches in neo-avant-garde conceptual art starting from the 1950s to the decade of the 1970s, which will be mentioned here, favoured an understanding of matter that is oriented to its intrinsic qualities and potentialities, and that augments its performative force. Connected to this, the artists favouring this approach started to develop at that time a non-auctorial position towards their own work, and elaborated processual works that unfold without a foreseeable outcome. As will be shown below, post-conceptual art in its turn responded to this radical loss of the material aspect of the object by creating a philosophical surrogate for it. It renders visible instead the processes through which the artwork could stage its own disappearance, by opening a space for those processes to be problematized.

Fluid, empty spaces in recent conceptual works, like the ones presented here, are connected both formally and methodologically to the legacy of minimalism. These works do not disintegrate into pure ephemerality, but fluctuate between visibility and invisibility in a processual approach. Documentation, which can be considered a historic device in conceptualism, is engaged in the works discussed here to shift the focus from reality and its experience to the processes through which reality is interpreted and valorized, and to explore how information is codified, or archived. Documentation is implied in these works to augment the material possibilities that a built form, a space, or a situation carries in the present and to create an expanded reality. In this sense, it performatively gives access to the virtual dimension of the presented facts.

The role of documentation in conceptualism

Tony Godfrey (2006) talks about the way the first principles of conceptualism show up in contemporary art nowadays. A new visuality has emerged beyond the initial puritan conceptualism. Along with it, painting has also come back into consideration, whereas hyperrealism and conceptualism can merge. In general a pluri-medial approach is dominating post-conceptual art. Godfrey identifies the connection to a context (in which the works are intervening) as a defining feature of this new conceptualism. He has launched, therefore, another term that would be more inclusive for post-conceptual art: 'Contextual Art'.

Documentation can function as a device that situates the object temporally and spatially reinforces its site-specificity. The neo-avant-garde of the 1960s which provoked the disappearance of the work in its original context, experimented as well with the complete abolishment of documentation, which was perceived as a means of prolonging the values of the market and its effects in a controversial art system. Documentation was understood as a factor that was impeding the work's capacity to be valued solely by their conceptual power (maintaining them materially), and therefore resituating them into a system ultimately foreign to them – the market. Michael Newman (1999: 214) shows that post-conceptual art, on the contrary, raised documentation as autonomous work. Newman regards documentation as a symptom of the crisis that conceptual art reached. Post-conceptual art simply makes visible the impossible processes of the disappearance of art, rendering visible and problematizing the loss of the object of art.

One of the most prominent theoreticians of conceptual art, Peter Osborne, even classifies emergent tendencies. He firstly identifies two types of conceptual art, 'light', as practised by artists like Sol LeWitt and Adrian Piper (taking into consideration her first works), and 'exclusive' or 'hard' conceptualism, practised by Joseph Kosuth and 'Art and Language' among others, which sustained a restrictive, analytical and philosophical position towards art. At a certain point the two domains coincided and art disappeared into the domain of philosophy, while the so-called 'end of art' could be proclaimed (Osborne 1999: 47–66). Kosuth's 'Art as Idea (as idea)', the title of a work of art and of his theoretical writing from 1967, expresses not only a tautology but also a self-referentiality of conceptualism that does not affirm a particular art object in its aesthetic dimension, but art as completely autonomous and self-referential.

Osborne identifies a third category of conceptualism that he calls 'generic conceptualism' that can be considered the generator of today's post-conceptualism. His example is Adrian Piper who works philosophically in her art, in the sense of producing works on her philosophical reflections, but her philosophical interest lies not in the nature of art but in various other domains, like space, identity and social presence, which she explores with conceptual means. This understanding of art permits, as Osborne argues (1999: 64–65), the inclusion of a plurality of media into art, as opposed to purely mental, strong conceptualism. This generic conceptualism, therefore, brought art to new forms based on the insight of the irreducibility of the role of the visual for artistic production. This reconfiguration of the object attracted the visualization of the processes of an actually impossible dissolution in post-conceptual art that became a constitutive part of the work.

In Sinta Werner's works, the clash between a virtual presence of architecture and its own documentation discloses an apparent fake. In her work 'Mise-en-cadre', shown in 2013 in Berlin, she photographs a real apartment block of Berlin Kreuzberg in juxtaposition with a model that she had built, by distorting the original. The truer and more enduring the model seems, the more liquefied and inconsistent the building appears. The cardboard model, which reproduces the original architecture of the first half of the 1970s as it warps it, reveals the process of the making of a fake. But at the same time, by their juxtaposition, it turns the original building, the centre of contemporary Kreuzberg life, into a scenography. The building method used by Werner is quoted from the setting of a film when a miniature landscape seems immeasurable due to its re-presentation in another media – film. This transposition in another media effaces credibly the border between real space and a bricolaged setting. In this case the model is not only copying or documenting, but also complementing and completing 'the real'.

Fig. 3.1-3.2: Sinta Werner, Mise en Cadre – Die szenische Auflösung, 2013, Kunstraum Bethanien, Berlin, ©Sinta Werner.

The model makes the original flexible, which finally matches itself to the size and the fake materiality of the miniature, until a symbiosis is achieved. Sinta Werner is cracking with geometric precision this apparent slipping of the original into its copy. She attains this by cutting illogical perspectives into her models and photographs. The viewer is confronted with his own inability to fuse the images and becomes an analyst of the collage, of the making-of it. Sinta Werner considers her own intervention in reality as an anticipation of the future[1]: every model is oriented towards the future, she states, as it represents an outlined project, and therefore a moment in the future, from which one can throw a glance onto a 'future' ruin.

Her models are accordingly incomplete, cut-out, partial forms that do not reach the totality of an ideal, an imagined prototype, and which dismantle what they hide: an absence.

For Michael Newman (1999: 206–221) the main difference between early conceptualism and recent post-conceptualism is the way the status of the object is treated. Whereas Duchamp selected a generic object that becomes art without being art, recent artists produce objects that become generic through the artistic act. Making visible the disappearance of the object is another way of maintaining it and situating it in another context. Quoting is therefore, in both cases, an essential approach that detaches an object from a context and transposes it into another register of meaning.

In the stop-motion videos of Yukihiro Taguchi (for example in 'Uber: Performative Skizzen', 2009), documentation is not a repetition of events in the past, but it makes the events possible in the first place. As Takeshi Hirata (2009) observes in an article dedicated to Taguchi's work, the film is not made with the usual stop-motion technique. Although the drawings develop the action in time, the result is not narrative. This makes the author call the videos 'stop-motion documentaries' since processuality and space are connected through this medium. The event in the videos emerges from the documentation of an action. Contrary to Carlos Bunga's use of documentation, documentation here does not fictionalize or modify an existing 'reality' retrospectively, but creates reality, transposing, in visual terms, an action.

The post-conceptual strategy of staging the loss of image and destroying representation (that is constantly used by the artists in this volume) is often connected to the disappearance of the object either into its function or in a generalization, in a type. In Taguchi's work in Lisbon 2011, he stamps paper with the textures of the city: the prints that the city itself leaves on paper reproduce industrially-produced objects and patterns. The prints are in this way both handmade, unique (in Taguchi's work) and serially reproduced (as the objects in the city). In this work the ready-made is at the same time a unique work, while the objects are maintained in their original context. Michael Newman (1999: 206–221) talks about these non-spaces in which a generic object is placed between a coded historic continuity and an innovation

Fig. 3.3: Sinta Werner, Mise en Cadre, 2010, Prokektraum Gerichtsstr. 67, Berlin, ©Sinta Werner.

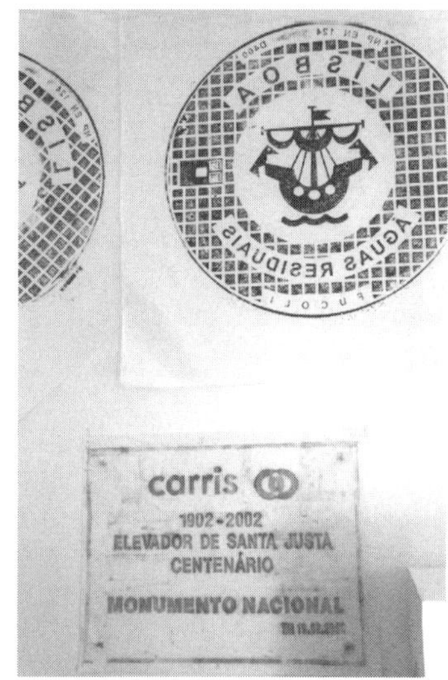

Fig. 3.4 and Fig. 3.5 (opposite page): Yukihiro Taguchi, 2011, Installation, Plataforma Revolver, Lisbon, ©Yukihiro Taguchi.

connected to the immediate present. In Michael Newman's view generic objects do not manifest any excesses, but maintain a certain perfection of form that is typical or representative of other forms. These objects are therefore neither manufactured (in the sense of expressing a personal sensibility), nor ready-made (which are appropriated or borrowed).

In his show 'Ordnung' (2008) in the gallery GDK Berlin, tables, bottles, chairs and brooms are *virtually* 'documented' by him in a video, which follows their functions in their original habitat, and establishes movement according to the relations that connect them in space. The virtual 'documentation' results here not from appropriation, like in the 'classical' ready-made, but from the generic object that is independent of any creator and possesses its own material force. This 'performative' force of an object that expresses the long history of its agency in space (with which Taguchi usually works) is a process that he calls *umräumen*.[2]

Conceptualism and materiality in the works of Zero

With reference to these preoccupations, the influential Düsseldorf group Zero, who only were active over a very short time span (1957–1966), formulated a fundamental statement. In their work they made an attempt at a reductive, abstracting purification, while not renouncing matter and its pure expressivity. In their work, matter appears as separated from external influences and human presence. Their work is also strongly connected to that of Yves Klein, with whom they collaborated, while their mutual influences built on personal connections and on common references to the work of other contemporary artists of the so-called 'Nouveau Réalisme', like Arman and Jean Tinguely, as represented in Paris by Gallery Iris Clert.

This new art created a break with modernism, dominated by the vision of Clement Greenberg that put forward an intuitive and sensitive cognition and gestual expressivity in painting. It also brought an anti-aesthetic, conceptual attitude that distanced art from the media-specificity proclaimed by Greenberg. Greenberg had identified the formal qualities of a work of art with the expression of artistic intention, whereas the meaning of the work was seen by him as lying in what the viewer could extract from what the artist had expressed perceptually (Greenberg 1989, 2000).

Heinz Mack and Otto Piene, the founders of group Zero, were working with drawings in smoke, images of fire and sculptures in air. As indicated in different biographies of Yves Klein (for example Berggruen 2004: 65–66), similarities between their work and that of Klein were later carefully separated out by both sides in an effort to mutually accept parallel phenomena, but to regard them as manifestations of different artistic attitudes and preoccupations (Berggruen 2004: 66). The processuality of creation is a common concern: Klein's experiments were seeking to expand the borders of art, searching for what art could be understood as spirituality. Klein is concerned with the figure of the creator and his subjective experience. Piene, on the contrary, shows more interest in the multiplication of the perceptual possibilities that painting offers. He and his colleagues in Zero intended an opening of the 'image' into unexplored territories, and detaching it from a creative will, while referring painting back to internal processes of matter. The manifesto of this loose group, which comprised around 50 members, was released in 1963 in the gallery Diogenes, Berlin. It can be regarded as being correlated to the desire for post-war moral purification in Germany, which formulated with simple technology a reaction against expressionistic and fascistic-connoted images. The manifesto outlines the search to attain a point zero and the serenity of a pure image without subject. 'Zero is stillness. Zero is the beginning. Zero is round. Zero is Zero'. (Zero 1963). Klein was both inspiring and inspired by Zero's work, as can be deduced by an exhibition of Klein, Mack (and other Nouveau Realists) in Antwerp 'Vision in Motion – Motion in Vision' (1959). The exhibition connected on a common ground the extreme radicalism of Mack's works with an investigation of a domain of interiority, specific to Klein's approach. In this exhibition Klein performed his famous act, during which he smoked a cigarette and exhaled blue smoke, while uttering: 'At the beginning there is nothing, after that a deep nothing and above that a deep blue'. (Berggruen 2004: 68). Klein's theatrical work is meant to create for the audience an ambience in which they can experience his personal scenography – a mix of his own music pieces, performances and a personal choreography with dancers, actors and himself.

At the same time, Zero presented a similar work at the opening of their group exhibition in the Schmela Gallery, Düsseldorf, which released also the first issue of the Zero-magazine (1961). Zero presented here their 'Luftplastiken' (known with the English name as 'Sky Art'), which consisted of performances with flying and luminescent bodies, and came close to Klein's aerostatic sculptures of 1957, the 1001 balloons he launched at the inauguration of one of his exhibitions in the Iris Clert Gallery.

In 1962 Zero created the Zero-Festival, which was meant to be an analysis of the point zero. The intention was to release a free territory in painting using pure elements. They showed sculptures of fire, of earth, of soap, of light, or moving light, such as fireworks. Gradually these events involved the audience more and more (Mack 1973: XXIII).

Otto Piene affirms: 'From the beginning we understood zero as a name for a territory of silence and new possibilities, not as an expression of nihilism or a dada-similar gag' (Mark 1973: XXIII). As a precursor of Fluxus practices, Zero worked as well with industrial seriality and intermediality. Their dynamic art (*dynamo* was a key concept for them) was also driven forward by Jean Tinguely joining their group. Even more than Klein, whose scenographic art was an expression of his own conceptual environment and figure, Zero shifted the focus towards a de-subjectified art that brings into being, or simply makes visible, intrinsic processes present in matter that emerge out of its natural kinetic development.

To situate recent post-conceptual approaches, the position expressed by Zero seems to make a fundamental statement in the sense of having traced a direction of thinking with ramifications to the present. While Zero's art stresses processuality and demonstrates a non-auctorial attitude to its own artistic production, Klein's art, in spite of striking formal similarities, creates spatial and *theatrical contexts of personal experience*. In this way he connects his own vision to the apperceptive effects upon the viewers. On the contrary, Zero fuses conceptualism with an attention to matter and its performative, *de-subjectfied* expression.

This line of thought is relevant for conceptual works like the ones presented here, in respect to the connection between conceptualism and a non-subjective attention to matter. As can be seen in the discussion below and as has been shown in the first chapter connected to performativity, the artists talk about their highly conceptual works, less as personal, abstract experiments, but as a way to provoke the manifestation of the forces that situations carry. Kubota, for example, explains that he is constructing the work according to the responsiveness of the material.

Conceptualism and materiality in the works of Gutai

Contemporary to Zero, the Japanese group Gutai constitutes for Carlos Bunga another significant reference (Bunga 2007 interview). In the vision of Gutai, art can happen at any time and can be ephemeral and contingent, or it can happen constantly. It can be the air, a sound, nature growing, an action or the lack of one. In this sense Gutai comes close to Zero since its members created a processual work that developed independently, detached from an author and following the laws of matter, which became visible, effective and brought processes into being.

Yoshihara Jiro founded Gutai in 1954 in Osaka under the name Gutai Bijutsu Kyokai (Gutai Art Association). The borders of the group were very flexible. Artists were continuously admitted to or were leaving the group. When participating in the first 1955, 1956 and 1957 Gutai exhibitions, however, their works were signed collectively – a strategy with non-commercial implications. It would require further analysis to determine whether this collective approach was due to Japanese old practice, in which an artist was identified not by his own subjective approach but by a school, a master and a particular tradition.

Gutai has been considered a precursor of the Nouveau Réalisme of the 1960s, in their work with body and with elements. Their work preceded the first happenings of Allan Kaprow, that involved the participation of the audience ('18 Happenings in 6 Parts' [1959]), the first performances of Yoko Ono in 1961, those of Carolee Schneemann in 1963, and the work of Joseph Beuys in 1958 with fat and felt. Gutai was making collective art, participatorial art, process art, performance art, and using, as well, the immaterial as substance for their work, such as air, water, fire, sky. The group's official French website, set up in 2001, and realized by Rena Kano, Michel Batlle, Ben Vautier and supervised by the Ashiya Museum Japan, contains a well-documented archive with texts and images to their work (Kano et al., 2001).

The recognition of the group outside Japan is mainly due to the efforts of Michel Tapié, who met the group in 1957 and introduced them to Allan Kaprow, who extolled them for their contribution to the domain of happening (Kaprow 1966). Regarding their influence, it has been questioned extensively (Restany 1982, Centre George Pompidou 1983, Duschek 1997) whether Klein, who was a fervent follower and practitioner of Japanese Zen philosophy and art and had been many times to Japan, was informed about the work of the Gutai Movement, or if he got to know about their work through the intermediary Michel Tapié and then transmitted it to the Zero group.

Shiraga Kazuo's work can be considered paradigmatic of early body art and performance art. In 'Challenge to the Mud' from 1955, he uses extreme bodily effort and force, painting directly with his body. Other artists concentrated more on action painting were Murakami Saburo, who was throwing colour on canvas (1954), and Shimamoto Shozo, who was painting directly with pigment, including the factor of randomness. Murakami Saburo was concerned with the destruction of the medium, but also with the architectural qualities of colour, surface and movement. In 1955 he installed a row of canvases and jumped through them in the 'Passage' performance, which was presented in the 1956 Gutai exhibition.

Equally innovative was the fact that Gutai rated the art of non-professionals the same as high art and included coincidence, accident and failure in the definition of art. Gutai artists refer in their manifesto (Gutai 1956)[3] to their actions of destruction and construction as means to discover the material qualities of space, situations and objects that they understand as transformative in time. This operational way of conceiving of space and art is described as a pictorial process, which extracts action from the potential of matter. Art was understood by them as non-art and art at the same time. Therefore, the chemistry professor Toshiko Kinoshita painted with the unpredictable results of chemical experiments, while her work became visible many hours after its creation. Generally the Gutai members were not interested in suggesting an interpretation to their multifaceted work and didn't title their work, which in this way remained open to various associations. As can be deduced from their manifesto (Gutai 1956), the group's actions and works were not implying common formal principles. Ahead of their time, they were also working with extreme experiences, like Shozo Shimamoto's performance in which the audience is asked to cross a shaking bridge – a work that is quoted in Gutai's manifesto (Gutai 1956) and that originates in a Japanese tale. Other works are striking pieces of land art, realized even before 1956, like Motonaga Sadamasa's structures of polyethylene filled with water, as well as smoke or water open air pieces, integrated between trees and geologic shapes. Atsuko Tanakas was another 'landscape artist' (although this concept is ulterior), who's work consisted of installing flickering light in various environments. Media specificity and seriality also preoccupied Gutai, with solutions that anticipated with almost a decade similar works done in the Euro-American context. Shimamoto created a portrait on film during which he kept a frame fixed on a character for many minutes, and Yoshihara Michio exhibited his painting not as an original, but instead projected on a screen. Appropriation art is essentially connected to these methodologies. At one of their group shows they picked up a piece of graffitied cardboard from the street and exhibited it in the gallery as an autonomous work (Takashina and Viatte 1987).

According to Shozo Shimamoto's website (Shimamoto, date unknown), in 1950 he was working with breaking both the surface and the material support of the work in his paintings with holes, while experimenting with the spatiality of the medium. Shimamoto explains that it was only later that he discovered the works of Lucio Fontana and their mutual affinities. Shimamoto practically introduced the dimension of time in painting while 'performing painting'. His experiments with sound, he understood rather as visual art than as music.

> Despite the word 'stage' our performances lacked any of the literary qualities of normal drama, and were limited purely to the presentation of art. Yet, they were presented on the stage, and were based on time; in other words, they were art that changed.
>
> (Shimamoto, date unknown)

The recognition of the work of Shozo Shimamoto in the Euro-American context was due firstly to a 1994 New York Guggenheim Museum exhibition 'Japanese Art After 1945: Scream Against the Sky' (Munroe 1994), where Shimamoto had been invited to represent the art of Gutai. The curator, Alexandra Monroe, made the discovery that the paintings with holes, which contained newspapers from that epoch, were from 1950, which demonstrated that Shimamoto's work preceded that of Fontana, which reversed the prevailing perspective on the periodization of the avant-garde. Shozo Shimamoto was invited by the Los Angeles Museum of Contemporary Art (MOCA) in 1998, to be represented in an exhibition on the art of the last century, in the context of the works of John Cage, Jackson Pollock and Lucio Fontana[4] (Nash, date unknown).

In an interview between Rossitza Daskalova and the two Gutai artists Yoshio Shirakawa and Masachi Ogura (Daskalova 1997), they recount that it is possible to talk in Japan about two avant-gardes: one that existed before the two world wars that was strongly influenced by European socialist movements and Marxist ideas and had to stay in the underground in the context of the official occidentalization that the Imperial House promoted. The other avant-garde, which was active after the world wars, had its origin in the controversies that were prepared by the first. The artists that could not show their work at that time now stepped into the limelight, in order to act directly in their social environment. These movements, which Gutai belongs to as well, brought a new confrontation with matter that demonstrates the influence of socialist discourse, connected with a genuine spiritual perspective, which was specific for the consideration of the object in Japanese culture. Gutai also represented a very early reaction to abstractionism (the name Gutai means 'concrete' in Japanese) and generated an overlapping of art and the quotidian half a decade before the emergence of Nouveau Réalisme with its similarly oriented name and project.[5]

Gutai's manifesto (Gutai 1956) accentuates a separation from the formalism and purifications of abstractionism, but also from the art of Dada to which it had been related. The difference that Jiro Yoshihara invokes in the manifesto in relation to abstractionism and Dada is mainly the treatment of matter. Ruins are for him a means to measure the decay, transformation and movements of matter. The emphasis is not on the individual dramatic performances or shows of the artists, but on their efforts to achieve the ultimate goal of reaching an essence of matter and bringing it to life. Yoshihara stresses also that the intention is not to intervene upon matter as an agent that would use matter as an artist's *material*, but on the contrary, the goal is to present matter as it is in itself: 'The spirit does not force the material into submission' (Gutai 1956). Yoshihara was calling for new works with a fresh vision by invoking the fact that art coming from past periods is not relevant for contemporary sensibilities. He pleaded for the fact that the material expressivity found in the beauty of ruining architecture or paintings can only reveal its force when free of the artificiality of human intervention. Ruins are seen by him as matter that has recaptured its original life (Gutai 1956). In their attempt to 'produce something living' (Gutai 1956), their art is replacing what they call 'the centripetal approach of abstractionism' with a centrifugal one, in other words replacing self-referential art, with art that is open to different contexts. The auctorial, psychic approach of abstract art, which results from 'individual abilities' is regarded by Gutai as being 'overwhelmed by the shape of space still unknown to us, never before seen or experienced'. Whereas Gutai are differentiating their approach in relation to this: 'Instead of relying on our own image, we have struggled to find an original method of creating that space'. (Gutai 1956).

Another influential thinker and artist in Japan in this decade was Okamoto Taro (1911-1996) who published his controversial book 'Today's Art' in 1954. His writings, which appeared shortly after Gutai was formed, build a theory of an art of the concept. Written at the same time as the work of Gutai, his book is promoting an art that is not illustrative, that does not stand for a system of thought foreign to itself, and that does not lay claim to art historical genealogy (Japan Visitor, date unknown). The art that he envisioned contained the dimension of time and was based on movement. The second edition of the book was only republished in 1996 in Japanese and retrospectively demonstrated his influence on his contemporaries. Taro had been a former student of Marcel Mauss at The Sorbonne and a friend of the French surrealists André Breton, Louis Aragon and Max Ernst. In his book he suggested an essential differentiation between the art of modernity and that of the avant-garde using the following criteria: whereas modernity created an art based on theory, selection and classification, the new art should produce an art which should not demonstrate anything for future generations, neither imitates its predecessors nor itself. Okamoto pleaded mainly for an art that contains movement and which is not easy to accept or to understand. Good art is for him one that forces its viewers to think (Okamoto 1999).

Ei Arakawa, a Japanese artist living in New York, extends into the contemporary thinking the legacy of Gutai and other theoreticians of the Japanese avant-garde like Okamoto Taro. His hard to categorize work can be seen as an homage to Gutai, since it consists mainly in re-staging situations that he encounters or constructing changing environments, while de-contextualizing ideas and objects, until they lose their identity.

His performances involve the audience, without directing them, and sometimes even without signalling that they have become part of his show. Meanwhile artworks of other artists step inside his work, while creating a collision between objects, gestures, and moments with a certain lack of coherence of meaning, but with a specific intensity. Various actions, small events, or sequences that transform the course of the events, deconstruct any attempt to build narrative content into these shows. His work mainly recycles, resituates and brings into circulation information, fragments of material items, as well as stereotypes of cultural objects into a sequential, non-linear time frame. Ei Arakawa is also constantly building, rebuilding, and un-building various configurations in which the human agency works as a casual motor force. In his performance 'Multilayereddisc', with Nikolas Gambaroff (2010), pieces of fabric, canvases with drawings, and papers with ink and drawings float around the exhibition space, while being constantly painted on the spot, exhibited and framed. In his 2012 performance series at The Tanks or Tate Modern, he used fragments of commercial 'performance' routine and of folkloric elements from Japan, while cross-quoting references and involving the audience in a visually stunning and apparently meaningless dance with objects. He was 'zooming out' of the happening and offering plural perspectives rich in artistic references, on the scene which was taking place. The motion that he induces in otherwise still forms of art, or in the process of contemplating art, is an essential device in his work. It can be seen in Arakawa's performance 'BYOF (Bring Your Own Flowers)' (2007) subtitled 'Live performance of painting-actions (not action-painting)', Lives of paintings in and out and in his 2012 show with Sergei Tcherepnin at the gallery Taka Iishi in Tokyo, in which he worked with other artists' paintings as the material for his amorphous shows. He calls this *rehearsal* or *market*.

In a 2008 exhibition in his gallery Balice Hertling in Paris, which was the outcome of a collaboration with the painter Nikolas Gambaroff and had the double title: '8864 3362 2250 Z1 CDGRT' (by Gambaroff) and 'TCCA Magazine 1' (a series of successive performances by Ei Arakawa), the two artists reconstructed the windows of the gallery in 1:1 scale, which nevertheless did not look similar. The frames of the canvas referenced the frames of the gallery windows and paintings from inside the gallery were transported and hung outside and in a neighbouring bar, accompanied by loud readings from newspaper announcements with an economic motive. The paintings were handed out from one visitor to another like an ordinary product, examined by the customers. Arakawa's aesthetic of half-formed objects and motions on the border of non-existence recalls Gutai's dictum of awakening life out of matter, and creating it in non-narrative but dramatic movements (Busta 2008). Natural processes, as in the work of Gutai, are put into motion while unpredictable arcitectural formations based on movement emerge, uncontrolled by the artist.

Arakawa's actions can be considered performative in Austin's sense, as an affirmation that creates a situation simply by being expressed, by taking place. This affirmation, the development of which stays open, is uncontrollable and unfolds independently of its author.

The critical distance – A conceptual principle

Leaving its traces in the post-conceptual approach, is what Hal Foster calls (1996: 29) *deferred action*. This term Foster develops in relation to the avant-garde in 'The Return of the Real'. It represents a possible key for the understanding of the way in which the early conceptualism of the neo-avant-garde (for example Gutai) has had repercussion in contemporary post-conceptual thinking, which is manifest in the work of Ei Arakawa described above and his method of 'collaging' historical material into the present temporality.

Historical and neo-avant-garde are constituted as a continual process of protension and retension, a complex relay and anticipated futures and reconstructed pasts – in short in a deferred action that throws over any

Fig. 3.6: Sinta Werner, Self Exposure, 2013, Photocollage, ©Sinta Werner.

Fig. 3.7: Sinta Werner, Milos II, 2010,
Photocollage, ©Sinta Werner.

Fig. 3.8: Sinta Werner, Milos II, 2010,
Photocollage, ©Sinta Werner.

Fig. 3.9: Sinta Werner, Scraping the Sky I,
2012, Photographic paper, ©Sinta Werner.

Fig. 3.10: Sinta Werner, Scraping
the Sky II, 2012, Photographic paper,
©Sinta Werner.

Fig. 3.11: Sinta Werner, Imperial Measurements, 2010, Installation view, 'Magic Show', Blackpool, ©Sinta Werner.

Fig. 3.12: Sinta Werner, Imperial
Measurements, 2010, Installation view,
'Magic Show', Blackpool, ©Sinta Werner.

Fig. 3.13: Yukihiro Taguchi, Moment, 2009, 5th Vento Sul Biennial, Curitiba, Brasil, ©Yukihiro Taguchi.

Fig. 3.14: Yukihiro Taguchi, Moment, 2009, 5th Vento Sul Biennial, Curitiba, Brasil, ©Yukihiro Taguchi.

Fig. 3.15: Yukihiro Taguchi, Moment, 2009, 5th Vento Sul Biennial, Curitiba, Brasil, ©Yukihiro Taguchi.

Fig. 3.16: Yukihiro Taguchi and Vladimir Karaleev, Fabric/k, 2010, Program Gallery, Berlin, ©Yukihiro Taguchi.

Fig. 3.17: Yukihiro Taguchi and Vladimir
Karaleev, Fabric/k, 2010, Program Gallery,
Berlin, ©Yukihiro Taguchi.

Fig. 3.18: Yukihiro Taguchi and Vladimir Karaleev, Fabric/k, 2010, Program Gallery, Berlin, ©Yukihiro Taguchi.

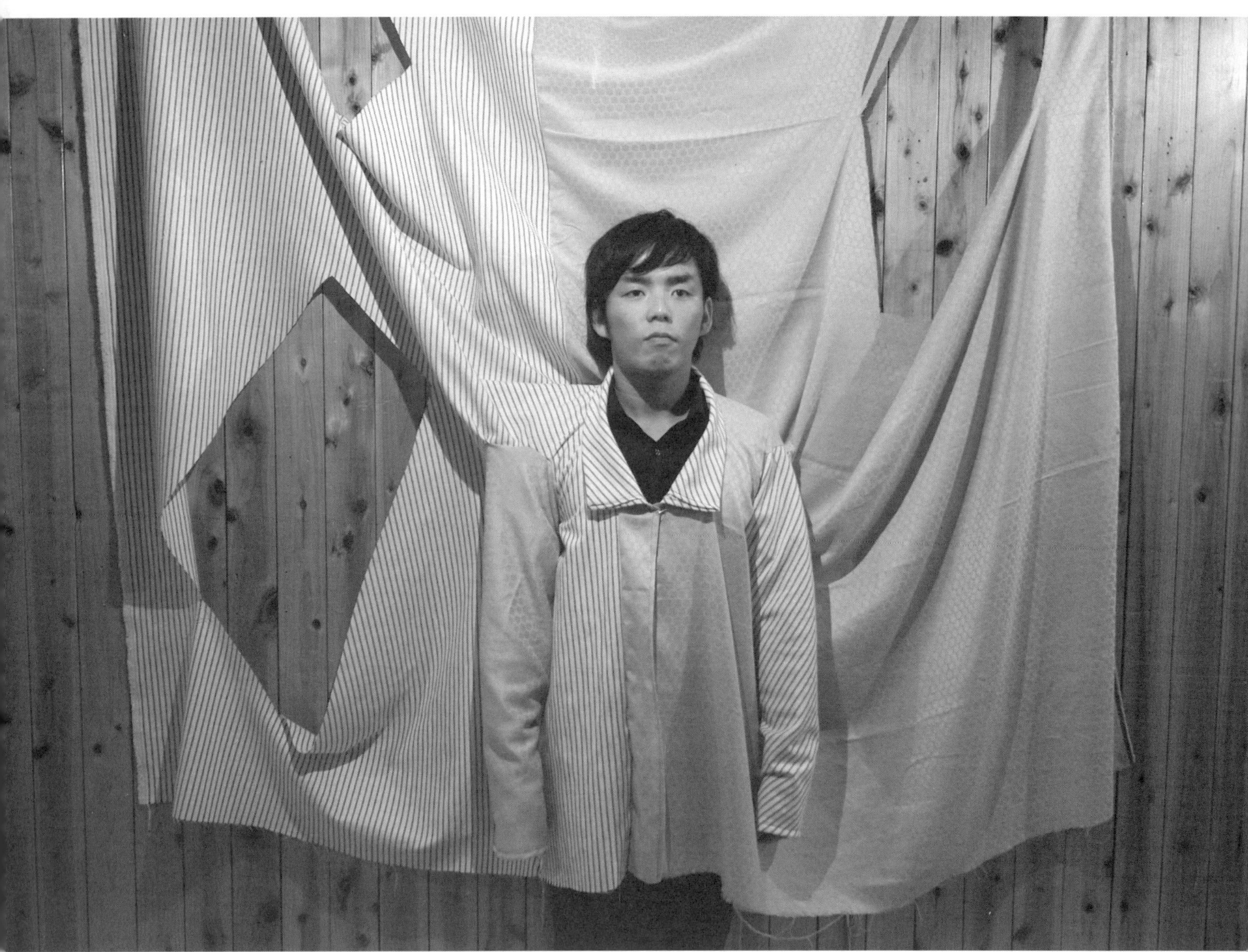

Fig. 3.19: Yukihiro Taguchi,
Fabric/k, 2010, Performance,
Tokyo, ©Yukihiro Taguchi.

Fig. 3.20: Yukihiro Taguchi, Fabric/k, 2008, Tokyo, ©Yukihiro Taguchi.

Fig. 3.21: Yukihiro Taguchi, Breakfast, 2009, Performance, Tokyo, ©Yukihiro Taguchi.

Fig. 3.22: Hironari Kubota, The Spinning
Idol Senjyu-Kannon, 2011, Centro
Cultural de Belem, Lisbon, Photo,
©Yukihiro Taguchi, ©Hironari Kubota.

Fig. 3.23: Hironari Kubota, The Spinning
Idol Senjyu-Kannon, 2011, Centro
Cultural de Belem, Lisbon, Photo,
©Yukihiro Taguchi, ©Hironari Kubota.

Fig 3.24: Hironari Kubota, The giant spin of fishing boat in Kitakuyushu, 2010, ©Hironari Kubota, Photo, ©Kazumichi Kidera.

Fig. 3.25: Hironari Kubota, The Worship of Mud, 2009, ©Hironari Kubota.

Fig. 3.26: Hironari Kubota, Illusory Race, 1999, ©Hironari Kubota.

Fig. 3.27: Carlos Bunga, Ágora, 2012,
Museu de Arte Contemporânea de
Serralves, Porto, Photo, ©Filipe Braga,
©Fundação de Serralves, Porto, ©Carlos
Bunga.

Fig. 3.28: Carlos Bunga, Habitar Color, 2008, Yuxtaposiciones exhibition, 2008, Elba Benitez Gallery, Madrid, ©Carlos Bunga and Elba Benitez Gallery.

Fig. 3.29: Carlos Bunga, Patrimonio Genetico, 2008, Yuxtaposiciones exhibition, 2008, Elba Benitez Gallery, Madrid, ©Carlos Bunga and Elba Benitez Gallery.

Fig. 3.30: Carlos Bunga, Rojo Solintor, 2008, Yuxtaposiciones exhibition, 2008, Elba Benitez Gallery, Madrid, ©Carlos Bunga and Elba Benitez Gallery.

Fig. 3.31: Carlos Bunga, Ruins Project, 2008, Site-specific installation, Art Unlimited, Art 39 Basel, Switzerland, ©Carlos Bunga and Elba Benitez Gallery.

Fig. 3.32: Carlos Bunga, Collective Memory, 2010, Sand, Carrara, Italy, ©Carlos Bunga.

Fig. 3.33: Sancho Silva, Effigiae Sapo, 2012, Effigiae exhibition, Kunsthalle Lissabon, Lisbon, ©Sancho Silva.

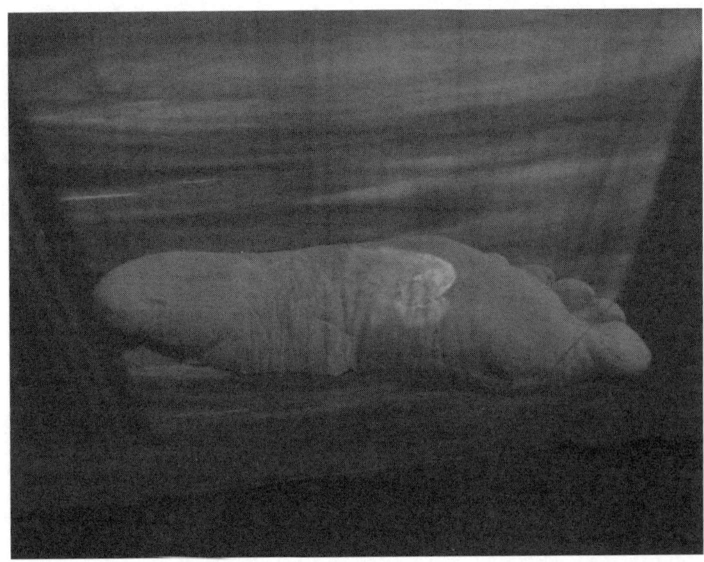

Fig. 3.34: Sancho Silva, Effigiae Sapo, 2012, Effigiae exhibition, Kunsthalle Lissabon, Lisbon, ©Sancho Silva.

Fig. 3.35: Sancho Silva, Effigiae Osga Coxa, 2012, Effigiae exhibition, Kunsthalle Lissabon, Lisbon, ©Sancho Silva.

Fig. 3.36: Sancho Silva, Effigiae Polvo, 2012, Effigiae exhibition, Kunsthalle Lissabon, Lisbon, Photo, ©Bruno Lopes, ©Sancho Silva.

Fig. 3.37: Sancho Silva, Scotoma, 2009,
Installation, Camera obscura, Kunsthalle
Bern, ©Sancho Silva.

Fig. 3.38: Sancho Silva, Scotoma, 2009,
Installation, Camera obscura, Kunsthalle
Bern, ©Sancho Silva.

Fig. 3.39: Sancho Silva, Scotoma, 2009,
Installation, Camera obscura, Kunsthalle
Bern, ©Sancho Silva.

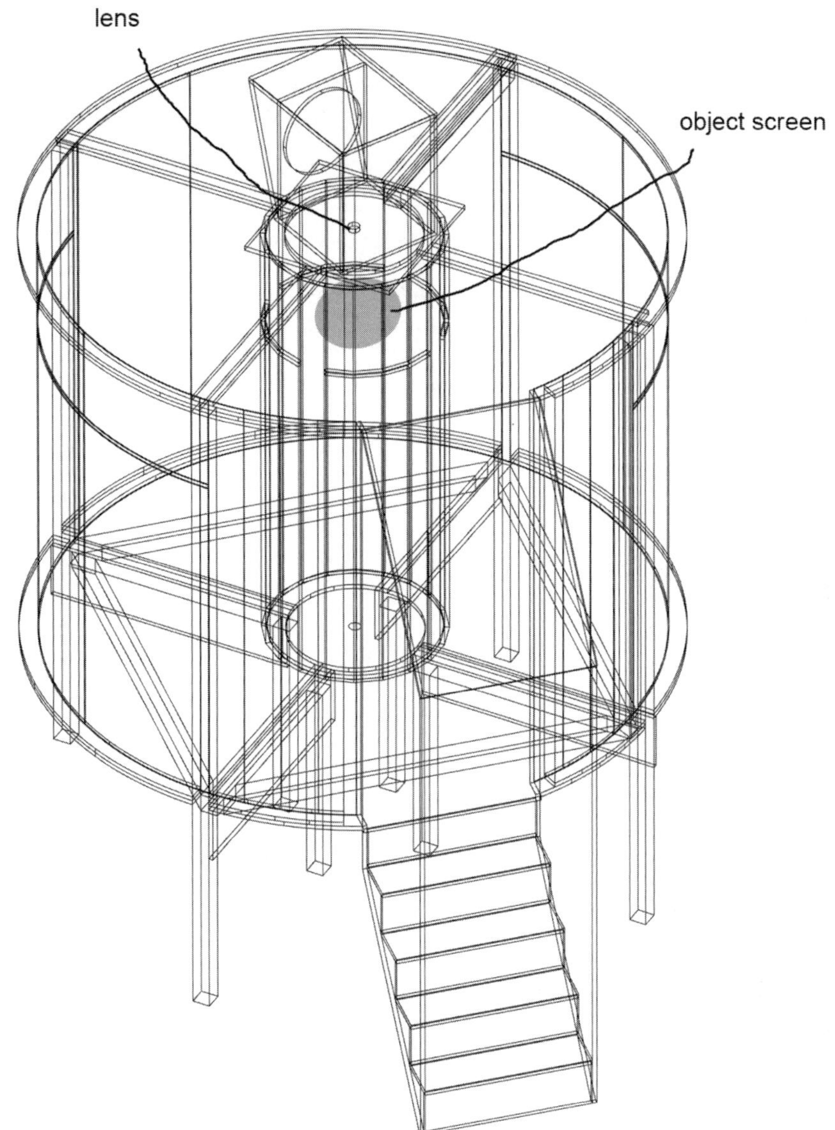

Fig. 3.40: Sancho Silva, Scotoma, 2009, Installation, Camera obscura, Kunsthalle Bern, ©Sancho Silva.

Fig. 3.41: Cristian Rusu, Horse Descending Monument, 2012, Model 1: 10, Exhibition view 'De la Matematică până în China', Salonul de proiecte, Bucharest, Photo, ©Cristian Rusu, ©Cristian Rusu, Salonul de Proiecte and Galeria Plan B.

Fig. 3.42: Cristian Rusu, Pavillon Tyrol, 2007–2008, Model concrete, Photo, ©Cristian Rusu ©Cristian Rusu and Künstlerhaus Büchsenhausen Innsbruck.

Fig. 3.43a: Christian Rusu, Calle de la Morte, 2008, film still.

Fig. 3.43b: Cristian Rusu, Calle della Morte, exhibition view – Space Itself, Galeria Plan B, Berlin, Photo, ©Cathleen Schuster, ©Cristian Rusu, Galeria Plan B.

Fig. 3.44: Cristian Rusu, Space Drawing, 2011, Plataforma Revolver, Lisbon, ©Cristian Rusu.

Fig. 3.45: Cristian Rusu, Triumphal Arch, 2010-on going, Sketch, Drawing, Collage, ©Cristian Rusu.

Fig. 3.46: Cristian Rusu, The Semicircular Pavilion, 2010-2012, Model 1:25, ©Cristian Rusu.

Fig. 3.47: Cristian Rusu, The Mountain's
Arena, 2010-on going, Drawing,
©Cristian Rusu.

simple scheme of before and after, cause and effect, origin and repetition.

(Foster 1996: 29)

In the participatory art of an artist like Ei Arakawa and in the body of the works described in this volume what Foster (1996) called the *critical distance* is an essential approach: the framing process in which, culturally and politically, the distance between the subject and the cultural context is constantly set. Foster comments on the different revivals of the avant-garde which culminated in a rediscovery of the real. The way the subject is set in these works and in other similar approaches, is not according to a linear framework. Parameters of identity and the fluctuating social and political context, which is formulated in these works, can be explained by Foster's model of "deferred action". Foster talks about inconsistencies of the different waves of the avant–gardes. These are nevertheless constantly reloaded and incorporated through later waves, which subsequently can assimilate aspects that were not followed up in the first place. This model can be applied to the agency of the performative work, which reassesses thereafter the historical legacy of the avant–gardes.

The broken identity of the conceptual work

In Hironari Kubota's spinning cars, boats and idols, he joins the iconography and symbolism of Shinto objects of worship with movement, produced by retro and handmade industrial machines. This break in the iconographic context of the image also detaches the object from a temporal continuity, which belongs less to an immediate reality and becomes rather a 'representation'. These are devices used in conceptual art since the neo-avant-gardes and, in the following pages, they will be brought into connection with a new attention to the so-called overlapping of the virtual and the real practised in recent art.

For Hironari Kubota (2011 interview), the fact that he is spinning a *reproduced* Buddha statue (one that he constructed himself), is essential to the understanding of his work. He confesses that what mainly interests him is not the original religious context of the statue, but its capacity to to become a polymorphous image and to be represented in affiliation with other contexts.

What I find most interesting is the fact that no matter what object is spun, the effect of its fast spinning is transcending the object and its image into something else, which becomes unrecognisable. I want to provoke that moment of experience in which people, carried away by confusion, see something else in this object. [...] While spinning the idol I change the speed and pitch of the music and this causes people to perceive the work and its environment differently. In that sense, my work might entail the act of turning time or 'changing' time, as if time slipped.

(Kubota 2011 interview)

As can be deduced from this interview, Kubota also considers the object as an accumulation in time of all the thoughts, beliefs, representations, and emotions of its users. These form the identity of the object for him, and it is this virtual identity of the object (real, but not actual in the immediate present) that takes to the surface in his performances.

This essential rupture in the continuity of the work of art and a work of art in which the unexpected event is a part of, but also a condition of, its appearance was first identified at the beginning of the 20th century by Walter Benjamin as a symptomatic phenomenon of modernity (Benjamin 1936: XIV). Benjamin considers a work based on shock and break as an effect of technology that interrupts and then again releases the flow of time and the continuity of space in representation. This new object of representation and its new media also determine discontinuity and repetition in experience. The art object is this way seen not any more as an object but an event, which determines that the viewer assimilates it through the experience of contingency, break and shock. Viewing is now being a part of it. The viewer is now exposed to alternative and simultaneous modes of representation which enter into his daily experience and from which he cannot detach himself. Therefore, for Benjamin, the modern experience of art is, due to its technological modes of representation, a traumatic experience of reality. At the same time, for Benjamin, it is precisely through this unnatural experience that the viewer can develop a reflexive and critical awareness relative to the work.

> From an alluring appearance or persuasive structure of sound the work of art of the Dadaists became an instrument of ballistics. It hit the spectator like a bullet, it happened to him, thus acquiring a tactile quality. It promoted a demand for the film, the distracting element of which is also primarily tactile, being based on changes of place and focus which periodically assail the spectator. Let us compare the screen on which a film unfolds with the canvas of a painting. The painting invites the spectator to contemplation; before it the spectator can abandon himself to his association. Before the movie frame he cannot do so. No sooner has his eye grasped a scene than it is already changed. It cannot be arrested. Duhamel, who detests the film and knows nothing of its significance, though something of its structure, notes this circumstance as follows: 'I can no longer think what I want to think. My thoughts have been replaced by moving image'. The spectator's process of association in view of these images is indeed interrupted by their constant, sudden change. This constitutes the shock effect of the film, which, like all shocks, should be cushioned by heightened presence of mind. By means of its technical structure, the film has taken the physical shock effect out of the wrappers in which Dadaism had, as it were, kept it inside the moral shock effect.
>
> (Benjamin 1936: XIV)

Following Benjamin, we can recognize the art object of the contemporary era, as not only a result of representation, *but as a producer of its own reality*. It is therefore an object that produces the means through which it can be critically absorbed. The indeterminacy of time and space creates an art object that is contingent and performative in the sense that it is setting into motion its own conceptual deconstruction. A critically-aware audience that gives art an analytical reception has been taken to the extreme in the digital era, so that the thoughts of the viewer can now shape the trajectory of the work in a concrete way.

The conjunction between the destruction of the visual continuity of the image and the consequent performative approach in the art of the avant-garde of modernity, which Benjamin talks about, can be connected to the lost integrity of the image that was actually shaped by the political contexts of the time. Hanno Ehrlicher (2001) refers in his book 'Die Kunst der Zerstörung. Gewaltfantasien und Manifestationspraktiken europäischer Avantgarden' to the scenographic-militant fantasies and theatrical visions of the avant-garde as utopic discourses determined by new military and media techniques used during the world wars. The often destructive force of the manifestos stated in the period 1910-1939, bestow an authoritative force upon the image, which is regarded by Ehrlicher as their performative power.

Complete destruction of the image: Iconophobia

The interruption of a cultural continuity and effacing until a completely voided object of art is attained have a long tradition in the history of art. *Iconophobia* had an early history connected to the destruction of the ritual image of 'the other". Up to contemporaneity, destruction is a form of representation. It produces certain modes of critical experience. The viewer of destroyed art is conferred an ambivalent position: he is included in the event of the work, by the force of the destructive event that impresses him, but at the same time he is placed in the position of a critical observer and witness. The reproduction/documentation of the event of destruction has the ritual capacity to recreate the event anew, in every act of reception.

Destruction is a form of momentary interaction with the arduous and long process of building a cultural object and fixing its symbols (Gamboni[6] 2002). Destruction of art, by painting over or replacing a monument, an image or a religious symbol, historically, has been considered vandalism. Destruction is, in this sense, oriented towards objects as emblems and towards everything for what the object stands for. A destroyed image is in this sense a mobile medium of information transmission and can belong concomitantly to different discourses and ideologies.

The long history of destroying art is actually aligned with progress rather than annihilation: cultural heritage is destroyed to make room for a new ideal. Destruction, understood as appropriation, was also the weapon that the neo-avant-garde used against the classical avant-garde. In 1953 Robert Rauschenberg erased a drawing of the Expressionist Willem de Kooning. Now in the collection of the San Francisco Museum of Modern Art, 'Erased de Kooning Drawing' is considered the first neo-conceptual gesture.

Historically, the destruction of images is an attempt to deviate their initial functions and to reinvest them in new discourses that announce progress and frees space up for the manifestation of new ideas.

Destruction as a condition of the emergence of the new is alluded to in Carlos Bunga's video 'More space for

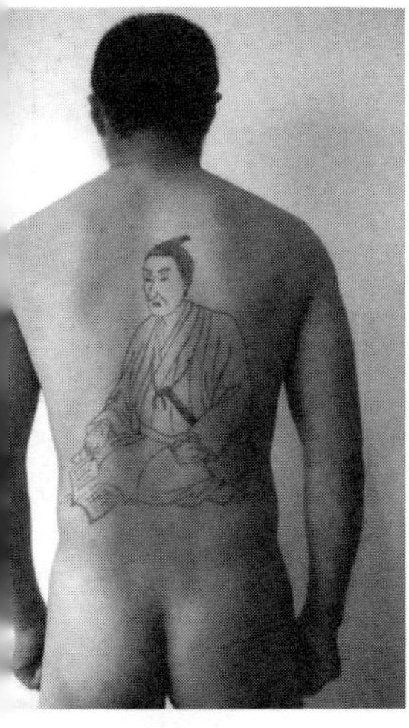

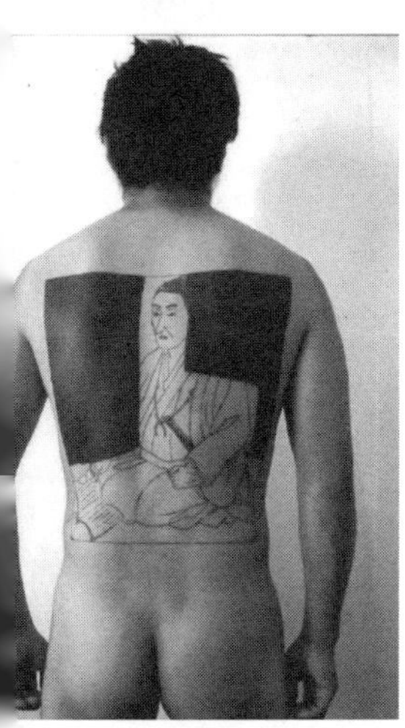

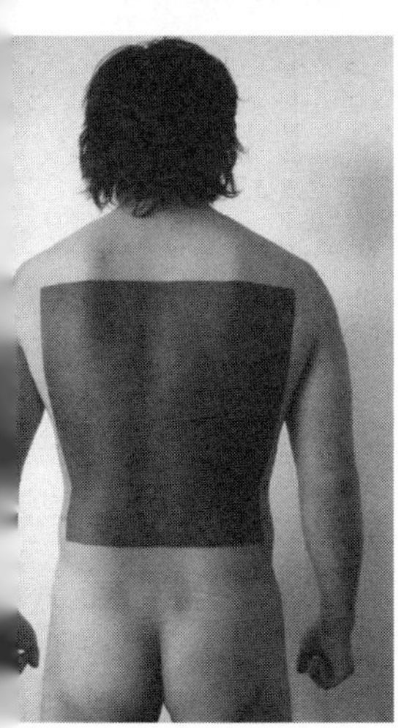

another construction' (2007–8), in which he destroys the images of some well-known pieces of architecture. In this sense, a destroyed image is more than an image in which an intervention has been performed, and is more than a hybrid. It is a new media that transforms the bi-dimensional surface of a reproduced image into a tri-dimensional object while at the same time incorporating its documentation. A destroyed image is in this sense one that carries the marks of the actions performed upon it. Bunga proceeds in a similar way in other works dealing with the instability of space. In his early experiments with glass, 'Lamp' and 'Bottle', he shows how he re-assembles objects that he had previously destroyed with a hammer. After the split of the spatial continuity of the object, the new objects re-assembled with tape attest to a new identity.

Much like the actions of Gutai artist Saburo Murakami in his early performance work 'Passage' (1956), Bunga perforated a painting, stepping inside and disappearing into the space of the actual painting. Bunga stages 'accidents' and processes of voluntary demolition, which are for him ways to study how the conjunction of space-time can be modified. On the other hand the jump into nothing has a long history in contemporary art and can be read as a somewhat fatal drive for nonsense or negation in artistic terms. In the case of Murakami, the artist's jump into the paintings annuls the finality, the justification and the consequences of his own artistic acts. While at the same time suicidal, provocative, social and philosophical, Murakami's act is also a statement of preservation. But freezing a sacrificial moment of loss becomes a mode to integrate one's art into a historical flow. In this way it ultimately leads to renewal.

In the work of Hironari Kubota, the transformation of an image until its disappearance not only modifies but also mutates representation, while a certain uncanniness is transmitted as with any act of destruction of art. In his work ' The Smell of Mud II' (2004), the image of the samurai Yoshida Shounin, a historic Japanese figure, which the artist himself was embodying through his tattoo, is erased and covered with a black square in a sacrificial and prolonged performance. The destruction of this image goes through various stages and represents, at the same time, a form of abstracting the image of the samurai by minimizing his 'story' and reflecting on the subjacent void that exists in any symbolic form. Kubota is also initiating a polemic here against the ideologically-coloured instrumentalization of this historic figure by the extreme right in Japan (Kubota 2011 interview).

The void in conceptual curating

The void has been involved systematically in recent curating. Understood as an object of display, the void made extreme statements in the 28th São Paulo Biennale in 2008, curated by Ivo Mesquita and Ana Paula Cohen, but also in the no less famous 'Vides' (2009) in the Centre Pompidou, Paris. These 'non-exhibitions' followed the concept of void from very different historical threads.

Fig. 3.48-3.50: Hironari Kubota, The smell
of mud II, 2004, Tattoo, ©Hironari Kubota.

In a mix of curatorial nihilism and insufficient financial support that left the largest part of the exhibition space empty, the 28th Biennial opted for a predominantly theoretical approach that replaced works with texts, publications and documentation of other works. The curatorial statement stresses the need to stop production, take a moment of reflection on the functions and possibilities of a Biennial for the contemporary world, and to meditate on the overproduction dominating the art market and the possibility of surpassing inconsistency. Partially received as a missed chance to offer visibility to various local artists in an international context, it was also seen as a refusal to support emerging artists. Still, prominent artists, the usual guests of international fairs and art events, were invited there too to complement 'the void' with various interventions and secondary events, which was seen in the local context as an attempt to back up the curatorial proposition.

On the contrary, for the group of curators, Laurent Le Bon, John Armleder, Mathieu Copeland, Gustav Metzger, Mai-Thu Perret and Clive Phillpot, the 2009 'Void' exhibition in the Centre Pompidou consisted in the archiving of past works with void, as connected to the conceptual and minimal tradition from the neo-avant-garde to contemporaneity, stressing, in a visual manner, its material expressivity and physical presence. Starting with Yves Klein's show in the Galerie Iris Clert (1958) and Robert Barrys's 'Some places to which we can come, and for a while be free to think about what we are going to do' (Marcuse) (1970), the void has also been presented as a way to point to the exhibition space itself, like in 'The Air-Conditioning Show' of Art & Language (opened in The Visual Arts Gallery, New York, 1972). The void can be also understood as a cessation of all artistic activities, as in Laurie Parsons' 1990 exhibition in the Lorence-Monk Gallery. Whereas in Maria Eichhorns' work in the Kunsthalle Bern (2001), the empty exhibition became a means of investing her exhibition budget into the restoration of the Kunsthalle itself.

In the following group of interviews the issues that have been referred to above are present. The discussions circle around the means by which each of the artists uses documentation as a creative device in his work and the way conceptual approaches have as a consequence the loss of qualities of the objects and bring up perspectives, which are not congruent with the logic through which an object functions, like accidents and gaps of understanding. The interview partners talk about the works rather as incomplete structures, results of unstable situations, and what *remains* after unwinding certain processes. •

Fig. 3.51: Hironari Kubta, A man in the sea of Japan, 2006.

Interviews

Interview with Carlos Bunga, March 2009

Q: Please tell me about your collection of old postcards in which urban disasters are documented. What is the function of documentation for you in this context?

C.B.:   In getting into contact with accidents and disasters, I perceive their intensity from a temporal perspective. The bombs in the world wars accelerated the temporality of the city. Temporality is measurable in materiality. Time and perishability are developing continuously, constantly, but we cannot grasp this continuity, we do not have consciousness about it. We can grasp it only through particular moments in this process of flow. I see mortality as a process through which things change and dissolve, little by little, but a catastrophe happens suddenly and it changes essentially this constant rhythm of degradation and accelerates it.

Q: Your work is capturing this accident as a moment of consciousness?

C.B.:   We have in our bodies (and all objects have) a material record of temporality, but when time gets accelerated, then it becomes more visible and it becomes concentrated in a moment. It is like the experiment of recreating the big bang: a possibility of recreating the past or accelerating time, till it returns to the initial moment. We can also think about inverting temporality, and that can be also determined through a process in which objects are involved.

For me the use of colour in my installations or objects also has something to do with temporality: if I use colour on the outside of the installation, it brings the installation into a spatial and temporal continuity with the gallery. After the construction has collapsed, the different colours on the inside walls of the installation suddenly reveal another temporality, which bursts into the other.

Q: You provoke the buildings you work with. Its outcome remains unknown to you as well? Is it this point of rupture from where you continue your work in any possible direction?

C.B.:   Yes, I don't have a concrete plan (like a model) from which I build everything. On the contrary, I also change the history of what happened and with it, its documentation. The lack of a model keeps different possibilities open.

Q: Your use of documentation covers a very broad spectrum. Please tell me about your exhibition 'Yuxtaposiciones' at Elba Benitez Gallery in 2008, and the different ways in which you work with documentation in other works as well.

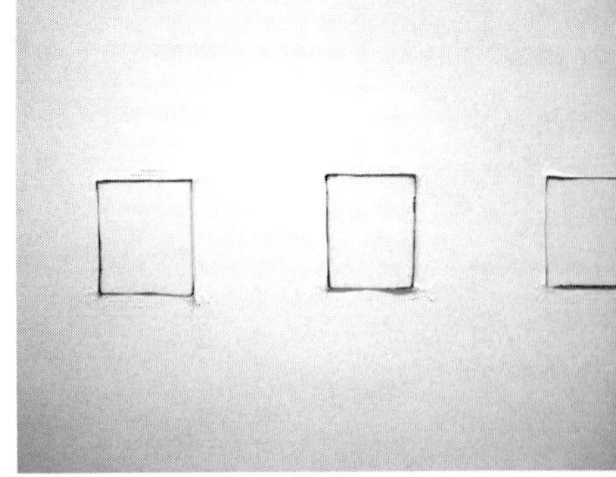

Fig. 3.52: Carlos Bunga, 3 Untitled Pieces, 2008, Yuxtaposiciones exhibition, Elba Benitez Gallery, Madrid, ©Carlos Bunga and Elba Benitez Gallery.

Fig. 3.53-3.55: Carlos Bunga, The Phaidon Atlas of Contemporary World Architecture, 2008, Exhibition view and detail, Yuxtaposiciones exhibition, Elba Benitez Gallery, Madrid, ©Carlos Bunga and Elba Benitez Gallery.

C.B.: This exhibition was meant to be an installation in its totality, which connects all the objects in space. The emphasis on colour, in its pure form as pigment, is meant to extend my architectural thinking on space. The pigments are for me recalling colour before painting, a virgin territory, and they carry and create a concentrated sense of spatiality. They express a returning to an original form of working with paint that comes close to a building process. Pigment is also a dynamic form, the slightest move changes its shape and the construction I made out of it can collapse any time. It bears as well this quality of fragility and changeability. As I started building this exhibition from the larger installation, the smaller works, with objects and pigments, are like a splitting into more concepts of the main idea of the entire installation. I was thinking of expanding all the possibilities that my large cardboard constructions are posing, and to analyse each of these possibilities in a specific way.

In the piece 'Between' in the 'Yuxtaposiciones' exhibition, you go through a narrow path that seems to be between two buildings and you get a strong perception of the space: the colours smell, the cardboard smells – my pieces have this very material component. It invites you to go inside, and then you find yourself in a space of *between* – it is not inside the gallery; it is not outside; it is an improbable space. It is, in a way, an abstract and concrete place at once. That is why I am working here a lot with contrasts as well: the small, pictorial pieces, which are exhibited on the wall, and this huge hidden space, which is parallel. I was also interested in compressing: in seeing what can happen if you compress the big installations into a slice, and the big installations into a mould of pigment.

I practised another type of documentation in 'The Atlas of Contemporary Architecture': I cut every page with a paper shredder, and then I stored the shreds in a glass box. This act of isolating behind a glass, and conserving pages from the history of architecture, was connected to the conservation of facts and figures from all over the world into a document that has to endure: an atlas, which you have in your house and look at [...]. By shredding it, I was intending to intervene in the functionality of that book.

Q: So it is also a way to deconstruct the image? You use the images of great architecture in your work and then you destroy the *representations* of them.

C.B.: Yes, that's the point [...] What I do is also to invert the process of construction, or just to deal in an abstract way with these constructions.

Q: And the result of the work in the *glass* box is like a painting. Again you transformed architecture into painting [...]

C.B.: Yes, the piece has some kind of internal, optical movement. When you look at it, it vibrates. You have to focus it in different ways. I am not working with destruction, or deconstruction for destroying, it is meant, rather, for inducing a transformation.

In this same exhibition, due to my interest in the appropriation of space, I have also put a table upside down. This time a domestic object is placed in an unfamiliar way. It tries to be part of the architecture (the gallery space) but succeeds, and does not succeed, at the same time. It is, and it is not, a table. I have called this series of chairs/tables 'Models', and I have exhibited them in the group exhibition 'Unmonumental: The Object in the 21st Century' in the New Museum, New York in 2008. It is about this permanent movement of concepts: what is a chair, a table? It is a chair, but it can also become something else, and it moves into something else.

Q: Recently there have been many exhibitions connected to the void. Could you please talk about the way you work with the void in your work, regarding also references to avant-garde preoccupations with empty space.

C.B.: My experiments with space have often been related to the work of Yves Klein. But what I am mostly interested in is to see how the same questions can be posed from other perspectives. To see how the social and political context of Yves Klein, for example, changed the reason why a question is asked, even if it is the same question, or, indeed, the way that it is answered. Also one more important thing for me is that these pigments are toxic: you cannot smell them, so I have put them in this acrylic box. This causes different problems: this precious, toxic substance, which is not only the spiritualist pure territory of joy, but has to bear something of the toxicity and surplus of production nowadays. Colour is a way to hide the transformations of matter in time, but it also bears a duality, since it is a moment of toxicity and destruction. So for me it is a means of questioning the instability of form and meaning, as in my big installations.

Let us also think about the recent Sao Paulo 28th edition 'Biennial' (2008) and the 'Voids' Pompidou Exhibition in 2009. These shows reconsider the idea of the void, but it is very much connected with a contemporary crisis of visuality, not with a formal experiment on the potentiality of some materials, or on the limits of art. If we do this split in the usual visual vocabulary, we create a moment of return to a state where we can think again about art, and this will be completely different to the effects that Klein's experiments had. The political environment has changed. There are also moments in the development of an artist, when everything must be kept in a state of unpredictability. If you start questioning your own development on a formal basis, and always in relation to artists from other historical periods, your own work becomes channelled in a pertinent, but predictable and uncreative way. The answers for these questions only come when many internal connections are carefully followed up. The first time I saw the work of Gordon Matta Clark, I stopped my work. I asked myself: 'what's the point'? This became so very problematic for me that I started to study Matta Clark seriously. In his work what was very interesting for

Fig. 3.56: Carlos Bunga, Yuxtaposiciones
exhibition view, 2008, Elba Benitez
Gallery, Madrid, ©Carlos Bunga and
Elba Benitez Gallery.

me was that he had a background as an architect, had worked in real estate companies, and that he always intervened in very socially-marked urban configurations of cities. I think for him, as opposed to me, the concern is very much about habitation, the social conventions of habitation, the urban changes in America at that time and the bourgeoisie of that period. These were his points of origin. He always worked during the last days of the existence of a house. He worked with its history, with the time before it was destroyed by the state and with the house as social identity.

I, on the contrary, am interested in space, not in habitation – as practice. I am interested rather in building simulacra of built spaces.

For me, creating documentation of my own work, like stills from a performance, or printing huge details of the works and selling them as pieces for collectors, is out of question. For work like mine, the documentation has to make a specific statement that can enlarge the understanding of the work.

Interview with Yukihiro Taguchi, July 2009

Q: In your work 'The Last Chair' (2008), the way you construct reality is by using documentation. Is this a common procedure you are working with?

Y.T.:   My work 'The Last Chair' has as its point of departure the idea of borders. When an object is divided and the pieces are again divided in an infinite process, you reach certain particles, until matter gets to a fluidity in which there are no more borders. I am interested in the visibility of these borders between objects, and which relations between objects create which type of borders. If we lay a fabric on distinct objects, it fluidizes their contours and their limits. Names and denominations also create limits. And what I am trying to investigate in my works are these territories that are beyond naming. I am trying to work with the laws that structure reality, and not with the reality itself, to work with gravity, for example, to let it have an active role in a certain situation that I create. By doing this I also provoke jumps from one register to another of understanding space, for example through the stop-motion technique.

Q: Your work is paradoxical, in the sense that there are two strains: one is the dissection and documentation of the real and its principles, and the other is an illusionary manner of presenting reality, like in your stop-motion videos. What is the function of illusion for you in constructing reality?

Y.T.:   Illusion is important because we normally stay in illusion. For me this is connected also with humour, and in my films there is always a humorous effect, and people get involved in these films by laughing, which signifies for me the presence of illusion. But in my installations I try, on the contrary, to pass from one layer of reality to another, and these jumps are the reality with which I try to confront the viewer. The viewer experiences different realities at the same time: the installations that they see in the gallery, the

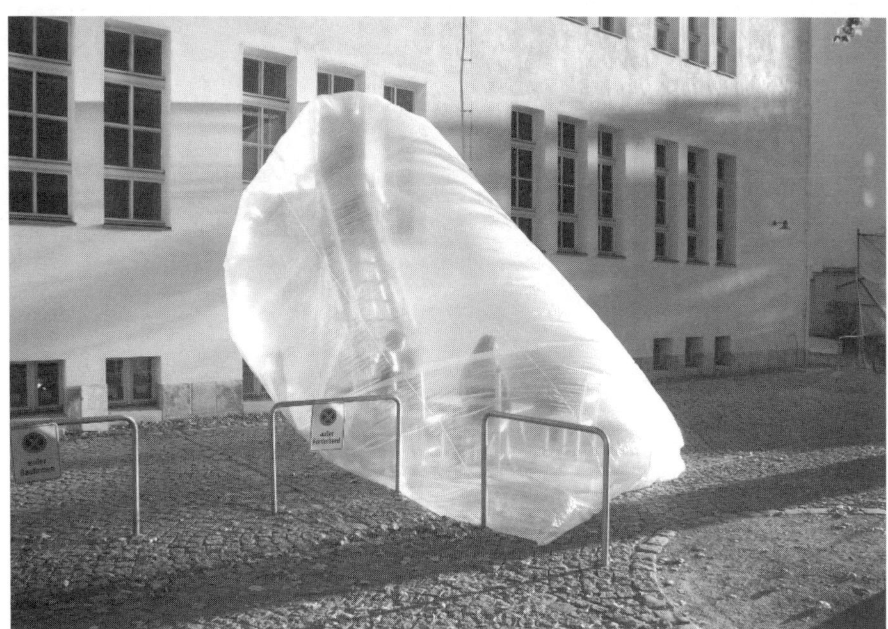

Fig. 3.57: Yukihiro Taguchi, Giftcafe, 2007, Berlin, ©Yukihiro Taguchi.

Fig. 3.58: Yukihiro Taguchi, Giftset, 2007, Berlin, ©Yukihiro Taguchi.

Fig. 3.59-3.60: Yukihiro Taguchi , Moment, 2009, 5th Vento Sul Biennial, Curitiba, Brasil, ©Yukihiro Taguchi.

objects themselves, the film. And in these conjunctions, which have nothing to do with illusion, lies our confrontation with reality – a continuous thinking process.

Interview with Sancho Silva, April 2009

Q: You always use the most simple, analogical means of representation. You avoid even video, replacing it with a 'direct' image transmission – the *camera obscura*. Why is that?

S.S.:   I am not against video, but if you can do it in a simple way there is no need to complicate things, and each medium and mechanism brings another quality and characteristic of the image and they have other implications. The *camera obscura* is always immediate, what you see is real time, while the video can record. The *camera obscura* requires special conditions: it doesn't work at night and, with its simple device, we could consider it almost a window. Video can also be used like a window: you film something on the street and project it onto the wall inside: you form a window. But I always believe that it is easier to make an opening in the wall, and then you have a window. Different implications originate from the way you construct what you are seeing and how you interpret what you are seeing.

Q: By eliminating the possibility to record and then rewind an action, you stress that both vision and media not only distort, but also produce information, and this is both a critical position in relation to mass manipulation, but also an insight regarding the power of vision to establish reality.

S.S.:   I try to produce and present alternatives to the space-time to which we are accustomed, different spatial organizations and organization of time, as they implicate each other. I try to make you extract yourself from your usual space-time.

I want to see how architecture, the urban environment, or the eye, work as devices in this sense. This is also an effect of bewilderment, because once you are able to extract yourself from the eye or from the architecture, you can be disoriented. In my 2006 work, 'Kunstgriff', I have gone even further, in the sense that I eliminated both video and *camera obscura* and what I have kept is just the device of framing: two details that can be viewed and the rest, the painting, the room etc., is eliminated. On the other hand there is always the possibility of going outside the device and seeing the details in context, and the whole construction from outside. Then you can understand what happened in-between the fragments.

In 'The Museum of Light' (2008), I have placed the 'museum' on an empty lot in Montreal, which was for sale. The idea was to make a museum of light, in the sense of a device that makes a *reflection* of what is going on around it, a representation of what is happening in the neighbourhood. The neighbourhood had been renewed, there was a lot of property sales speculation and there were also lots of junkies hanging around. It was a very rough area, which was going through a lot of changes, and my work is an abstract reference to these changes through the medium of light. When I was doing the project there, two metres of snow was covering the lot, so I decided to do something with the snow, because it became like a glowing

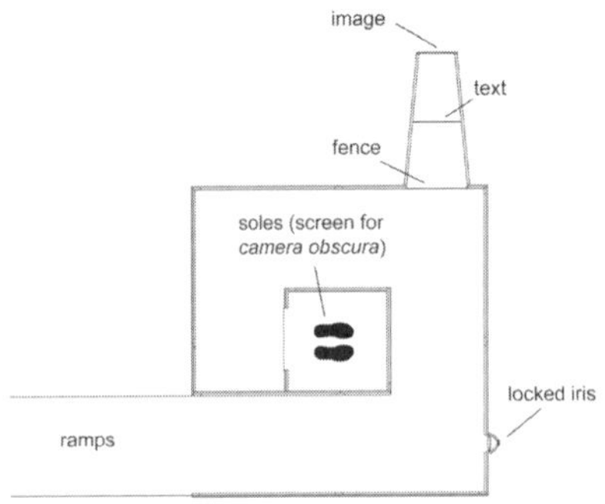

Fig. 3.61-3.62: Sancho Silva, Musée
Lumière, 2008, Empty lot by Ottawa Street,
Montréal, ©Sancho Silva.

sea of light when the sun was shining. The 'museum' was always changing its position, it was floating on the snow when the sun was coming out and when the snow was melting and it was supposed to last just until the snow was melting.

The art museum contained three different artworks: the first is an iris (which is made of a glass object locked with a combination lock), a locked eye that alludes to the idea of a riddle that has to be unlocked. The museum was a riddle of light and it was also an attraction point, and from the street you could see this shiny point in the building, a hook for the eye.

The idea in my work is to grab people into the spiral of the museum, into its dimension.

The idea of the hook has a metaphorical meaning: it makes you withdraw from yourself and see yourself from a distance.

The second work of the museum of light was the funnel (the cone) that is blocked at the end with a photograph. It is the photo of an old squat where people live in the summer; a shelter for homeless people in Montreal. Juxtaposed on the photo is text, which I took from a website advertising this area for the building of lofts. It is almost a poem for light. Set against the fence and the photography of the squatters' housing, it creates a contrast. I put up the fence as a sign of privatization of light – the aggressive side of this poem. I was also using a *camera obscura* as this is my habit now!

I placed a sign on the facade of 'The Museum of Light': *Beware of Electricity*, since it was a museum of light and it can electrocute you. People didn't know what this box-like construction was. It was this ambiguity and a fear also: 'maybe it is from the electric company and I can be electrocuted here'? But there was also a sign: *Museum Open 24/24*, so even at night, you could see some of the works.

Q: The technical configuration of your works determines that they are always responding to their environment. Beyond this technical level, how do you construct their *critical* site-specificity?

S.S.:   I like the way I can reflect the urban environment where the work is located. Also I like to reflect on the art environment. I reflect on a museum, as a machine of perception, that selects, eliminates, that emphasizes something. Museums are amazing machines. If you put anything in those conditions, it becomes a beautiful and important thing: through the pedestals, the lighting. In my works I am also playing with the idea of display, with the question 'what is a museum?' in terms of showing and selecting how a museum works as a mechanism and what it does.

Q: The different architectures that you build and the alternative visual devices that you propose are extracting the individual from his usual frames of perception, but on the other hand they are also compulsory. The devices you build are technical machineries that extend human faculties, but on the other hand conduct a multiplicity of possibilities into a pre-established direction for the visitor. Where do you intend ultimately to lead the audience, and what is your aim in this regard?

S.S.:   Architecture, or my constructions in resonance to it, is indeed very authoritarian. I am forcing the viewer to take a route, and the work is almost like a prison. Your path, your possibilities are conditioned, are defined. A city also defines your possibilities: you can go along the streets, but you cannot enter the houses. There are all these restrictions: there are things that you can see and things that you cannot see. The eye also works like that: selects by habit, by design, or by elimination. There are all these kinds of layers, starting with your conceptual apparatus, your ideologies, that filter and frame things and the skin of your body, and go up in scale to the layer of urban configuration and of geopolitical networks. There are all these framing devices. Wherever there is a frame, there is a possibility of you extracting yourself from it, like taking off your glasses and taking a look at the glasses themselves.

Q: Please describe also other means by which you approach vision in your works.

S.S.:   *Scotoma* means darkness in Greek, and is also a medical term that indicates the blind spot which we have in the eyes. In our eye, where the optical nerve touches the pupil, there is a black, blind spot, where we cannot see. As we have two eyes and each compensates the other, and also because the brain fills this gap with information from the other eye, we don't see the scotoma.

So my work 'Scotoma' (2009) is meant to visualize the scotoma. I have built a circular construction that I placed in front of the Kunsthalle in Bern where the group show took place, to make the reference to the museum clearer. Inside the construction there was a model of the eye with the darkness point in the middle of it: a ceramic ball, which received an image of the city projected onto it, and formed a *camera obscura*. But the ball had a distortion, so the image was also distorted, and there was also a blind spot where you could not see the city.

Q: Can you please talk about your works where you build hybrid objects? Which is their intersection point with design and its specific questions?

S.S.:   In my work 'Fragment', which I did in Hiroshima in 2008, I was searching for a *function*. It goes back to the same idea of trying to extract yourself from an environment, and is connected also to the idea that the city is over-designed. Wherever we go, everything is giving us an instruction on how we should move or use something. My installation, which has at its core an undefined fragment of an unknown object, exploits the same strategy with regard to use, but instead takes it in the direction of perception. Perception is more contemplative, and it also represents a mediation. It takes place on a different time scale from vision. The difference between perception and vision could be illustrated by that between the act of looking at a house and entering the house. The same thing happens in terms of use: as you walk along the street, or inside a house, everything is designed in a certain way, which you learn to decode by habit. If you see a chair you know how to recognize it, and it tells you how to sit in it. The way to use it, the instruction for how to behave and move in it, is always included in the object. My idea in this and other works is to try to create zones of ambiguity, zones where the message with the prescription as to how you should use the object is erased. Also I am interested in areas where there are no instructions, but this is not quite so easy, because when you have an empty space, and when you want to create a nothingness, it usually gets filled up with what is around it. It is similar to what the brain does with the scotoma. An attempt to create nothing has to

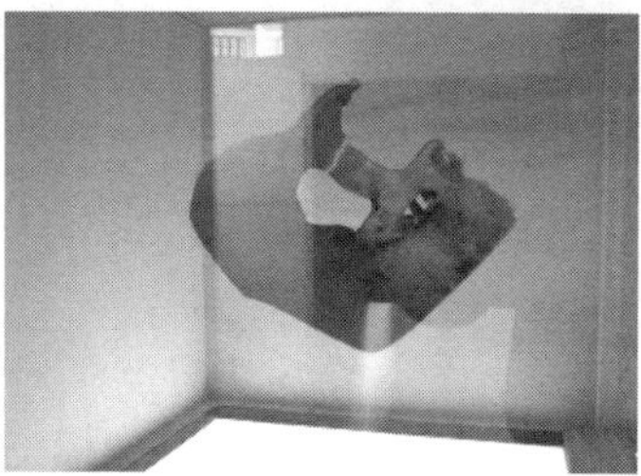

Fig. 3.63-3.65: Sancho Silva, Fragment, 2008, City Museum of Contemporary Art, Hiroshima, ©Sancho Silva.

be designed in a way that blocks the tendency for it to be filled up with other things that are in its environment.

I am trying out an exercise in dysfunctionality because I am trying to block something, and at the same time also open something, and this is precisely the language of design. More than that, I try to leave the prescription open for something unexpected to happen. In 'Fragment' there are no distinctions between the wall, the ceiling, the floor, the seats and the windows. There is this interchangeability of functions: the carpet is both on the ceiling and on the wall. Inside 'Fragment' there is this undefined object that is also connected to the idea of a museum, but it is more of a riddle. It is actually a fragment of a car that I found one day in Hiroshima, and it connects as well with the museum of Hiroshima, in the environment of which the entire piece was placed. The whole construction is reflected back into this fragment of something else, with something missing, and becomes a museum piece. In this way the object is a counterpart to the architecture. In this work I was mainly asking myself how to work with objects, rather than with spaces, with reference to the idea of interpretation, of *framing*. Objects are things you can hold and grab, whereas spaces are things that happen through time. You can see spaces in their state of destruction, or while you go from one place to another. Whereas with objects I am asking myself what influence they have on us: are they innocent, are they innocuous, do they work, do they shape us? How are they shaped? If you think of them in terms of space, objects are hermetic, but if you think at them in terms of function, they open up.

Space can also have functions, but an object has an opaqueness in a very literal way that space doesn't have. An object is something that you see whole, you don't see through it. You see it from the outside not from the inside, even though there are so many borderline situations. We can ask ourselves, for example, if a helmet is an object or if it is architecture? Also architecture can be seen as an object. The main point is this duality. A building that is rotating in 3D becomes an object. I want my work to move in this direction, into something I don't understand yet and want progressively to get to understand more.

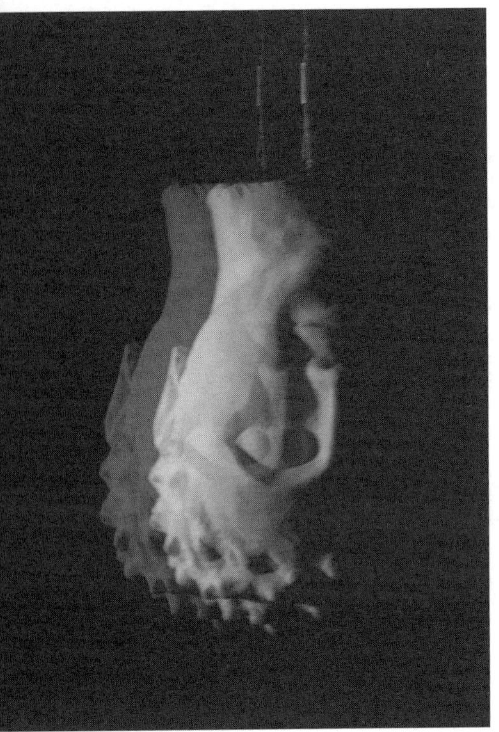

Fig. 3.66-3.67: Sancho Silva, Thauma, 2011, Plataforma Revolver, Lisbon, ©Sancho Silva.

Addendum

The Gutai Manifesto

With our present awareness, the arts we have known up to now appear to us in general to be fakes fitted out with a tremendous affectation. Let us take leave of these piles of counterfeit objects on the altars, in the palaces, in the salons and the antique shops.

These objects are in disguise and their materials such as paint, pieces of cloth, metals, clay or marble are loaded with false significance by human hand and by way of fraud, so that, instead of just presenting their own material, they take on the appearance of something else. Under the cloak of an intellectual aim, the materials have been completely murdered and can no longer speak to us.

Lock these corpses into their tombs. Gutai art does not change the material but brings it to life. Gutai art does not falsify the material. In Gutai art the human spirit and the material reach out their hands to each other, even though they are otherwise opposed to each other. The material is not absorbed by the spirit. The spirit does not force the material into submission. If one leaves the material as it is, presenting it just as material, then it starts to tell us something and speaks with a mighty voice. Keeping the life of the material alive also means bringing the spirit alive, and lifting up the spirit means leading the material up to the height of the spirit.

Art is the home of the creative spirit, but never until now has the spirit created the material. The spirit has only ever created the spiritual. Certainly the spirit has always filled art with life, but this life will finally die as the times change. For all the magnificent life that existed in the art of the Renaissance, little more than its archaeological existence can be seen today.

What still keeps that vitality, even if passive, may be primitive art or the art created after Impressionism. These are things in which either, due to skilful application of the paint, the deception of the material had not quite succeeded, or else, like Pointillist or Fauvist, those pictures in which the materials, although used to reproduce nature, could not be murdered after all. Today, however, they are no longer able to call up deep emotion. They already belong to a world of the past.

Yet what is interesting in this respect is the novel beauty to be found in works of art and architecture of the past, which have changed their appearance due to the damage of time or destruction by disasters in the course of the centuries. This is described as the beauty of decay, but is it not perhaps that beauty which material assumes when it is freed from artificial make-up and reveals its original characteristics? The fact that the ruins receive us warmly and kindly after all, and that they attract us with their cracks and flaking surfaces, could this not really be a sign of the material taking revenge, having recaptured its original life? In this sense I pay respect to Pollock's and Mathieu's works in contemporary art. These works emit the loud outcry of the material, of the very oil or enamel paints themselves. These two artists grapple with the material in a way which is completely appropriate to it and which they have discovered due to their talent. This even gives the impression that they serve the material.

Differentiation and integration create mysterious effects.

Recently, Tominaga Soichi and Domoto Hisao presented the activities of Mathieu and Tapié in Informel art, which I found most interesting. I do not know all the details, but in the content presented, there were many points I could agree with. To my surprise, I also discovered that they demanded the immediate revelation of anything arising spontaneously and that they are not bound by the previously predominant forms. Despite the differences in expression compared to our own, we still find a peculiar agreement with our claim to produce something living. I am not sure, though, about the relationship between the conceptually defined pictorial elements like colours, lines, shapes, in abstract art and the true properties of the material in Informel art. As far as the denial of abstraction is concerned, the essence of their declaration was not clear to me. In any case, it is obvious to us that purely formalistic abstract art has lost its charm, so that the Gutai Art Society founded three years ago was accompanied by the slogan that they would go beyond the borders of abstract art and that the name Gutaiism (concretism) was chosen. Above all, we had to search for a centrifugal approach, instead of the centripetal one seen in abstract art.

In those days we thought, and indeed still do think today, that the most important merits of abstract art lie in the fact that it has opened up the possibility to create a new, subjective shape of space, one which really deserves the name creation.

We have decided to pursue the possibilities of pure and creative activity with great energy. We tried to combine human creative ability with the characteristics of the material in order to concretize the abstract space.

When the abilities of the individual were united with the chosen material in the melting-pot of psychic automatism, we were overwhelmed by the shape of space still unknown to us, never before seen or experienced. Automatism naturally made the image that did not occur to us. Instead of relying on our own image, we have struggled to find an original method of creating that space. The works of our members will serve as examples. Toshiko Kinoshita is actually a teacher of chemistry at a girls' school. She created a peculiar space by allowing chemicals to react on filter paper. Although it is possible to imagine the results beforehand to a certain extent, the final results of handling the chemicals cannot be established until the following day. The particular results and the shape of the material are, in any case, her own work. After Pollock many Pollock-imitators appeared, but Pollock's splendour will never be extinguished. The talent of invention deserves respect.

Kazuo Shiraga placed a lump of paint on a huge piece of paper, and started to spread it around violently with his feet. For about the last two years art journalists have called this unprecedented method 'the Art of committing the whole self with the body'. Kazuo Shiraga had no intention at all of making this strange method known to the public. He had merely found the method that enabled him to confront and unite the material he had chosen with his own spiritual dynamics. In doing so he achieved an extremely convincing result.

In contrast to Shiraga, who works with an organic method, Shozo Shimamoto has been working with mechanical manipulations for the past few years. The spray pictures created by smashing a bottle full of paint, or the large surface made in a single moment by firing a small, hand-made cannon filled with paint by means of an acetylene gas explosion, etc., display a breath-taking freshness.

Other works that deserve mention are those of Yasuo Sumi produced with a vibrator or Toshio Yoshida, who uses only one single lump of paint. All their actions are full of a new intellectual energy that demands our respect and recognition.

The search for an original, undiscovered world also resulted in numerous works in the so-called object form. In my opinion, conditions at the annual open-air exhibitions in the city of Ashiya have contributed to this. That these works, created by artists who are confronted with many different materials, differ from the objects of Surrealism can be seen simply from the fact that the artists tend not to give them titles or to provide interpretations. The objects in Gutai art were, for example, a painted, bent iron plate (Atsuko Tanaka) or a work in hard red vinyl in the form of a mosquito net (Tsuruko Yamazaki) etc. With their characteristics, colours and forms, they were constant messages about the materials.

Our group does not impose restrictions on the art of its members, letting them make full use of their creativity. For instance, many different experiments were carried out with extraordinary activity such as art felt with the entire body, art that could only be touched, Gutai music (in which Shozo Shimamoto has been doing interesting experiments for several years) and so on. Another work by Shozo Shimamoto is like a bridge that shakes every time you walk over it. Then a work by Saburo Murakami that is like a telescope you can enter to look up at the heavens, and an installation made of plastic bags with organic elasticity etc. Atsuko Tanaka started with a work of flashing light bulbs, which she called 'Clothing'. Sadamasa Motonaga worked with water, smoke etc. Gutai art put the greatest importance on all daring steps that lead to an undiscovered world. Sometimes, at first glance, we are compared with and mistaken for Dadaism, and we ourselves fully recognize the achievements of Dadaism. But we think differently, in contrast to Dadaism, our work is the result of investigating the possibilities of calling the material to life.

We shall hope that there is always a fresh spirit in our Gutai exhibitions and that the discovery of new life will call forth a tremendous scream in the material itself.

(Proclaimed in October 1956, published in December 1956 in the art journal 'Geijutsu Shincho')

Jiro Yoshihara (Gutai 1956)

NOTES

1   In the press release of her exhibition 'Mise-en-cadre' (2013) in Kunstraum Kreuzberg Bethanien, Berlin.
2   A German term that could be translated into 're-spacing space'.
3   See appendix to this chapter for complete manifesto.
4   The term 'Action Painting' was launched in the December Issue of ARTnews (1952) by the art critic Harold Rosenberg. The term was used by him in relation to artists that regard the canvas as a space for action.

5   Gutai was founded in 1954 and the Nouveau Realisme Group was started by Pierre Restany in 1960.

6   As one of the curators of the exhibition 'Iconoclash, Beyond the Image Wars in Science, Religion and Art', which took place 2002 in ZKM (Zentrum für Kunst und Medientechnologie) in Karlsruhe, Dario Gamboni writes an introduction where he discusses historically the destruction of images (Gamboni 2002).

CHAPTER 4
Postdigital and the virtual: A question of density

The invisible under the medial screen

Centred around the preoccupations expressed in the interviews and in the works, this chapter navigates through various recent theories that built up the understanding of the virtual connected to technology, derived and independent from the digital. Conditions in which the experience of the virtual is possible are scrutinized.

The virtual borders on issues of visibility and invisibility. These are themselves a consequence of techniques of representation and an outcome of media. In a collected volume of philosophical essays dedicated to visibility, Dana Hollander (2002: 34–40) emphasizes the borders of representation. She comments on the relationship between the *punctum* of Roland Barthes and that which Jacques Derrida designates the invisibility of the border of representation, which for him is framed by the incommunicable and the non-verbal (from the perspective of the discourse). Hollander mainly discusses the texts 'Droit de Regards/Right of Inspection', which Derrida published about the photographic work of Marie-Françoise Plissart in 1985, and his quasi-autobiographical work *Mémoires d'aveugle, L'autoportrait et autres ruines/Memoires of the Blind. The Self Portrait and Other Ruins* (Derrida, 1991), which appeared on the occasion of a self-portrait exhibition with the same title in the Louvre in 1991. For his essay, Derrida selected a series of self-portrait drawings and prints from the collection in the Louvre.

In this text Jacques Derrida explores issues of vision and blindness and their relationship to representation, in relation to works that depict fictional, historical and biblical blindness. For Derrida, drawing is itself blind, as it is rooted in memory and anticipation and he shows that drawing substitutes mediated vision for direct sight. Derrida talks in this text about the *punctum caecum*, which is another term for *scotoma*, the object of Sancho Silva's 2009 work presented at the Kunsthalle, Bern. *Punctum caecum* demonstrates for Derrida that perception contains non-perception, and that the visible overlaps with the invisible until it reaches the point at which one contains the other. For Derrida the visible results from the discourse that was interrupted by itself. Derrida connects the *punctum caecum* with the *punctum* of Roland Barthes, which stays equally invisible and ungraspable.

In some of the works of Sancho Silva ('Mus Papilionoideia', 1996 or 'Film Machine', 2003), questions of visibility and representation practically construct architecture. The exterior world is projected by the analogue camera obscura inside architecture (in the gallery space or in a specially constructed pavilion in the middle of the urban rush), which becomes the device of observation itself. The resulting 'film' about the 'exterior world' is a real time succession of images that is extending architecture beyond its physical limits: the constructions are defined by the principle of a cinematic movement of image – 'the real' – which turns to be a part of architecture. Without using video or photo, his works transform reality into a representation by converting architecture into a *medium* of representation. Reality becomes credible only as it translates into another medium – through architecture – that both gives access to and blocks 'reality'. The position of authority that the viewer is conferred by the device is played out against the authority of the 'architectural machine'.

In 'Film Machine' (2003), he constructs a closed and dark architectural environment with an opening of a 35-mm frame, through which the viewer can observe the street in real time, creating a filmic experience of playback.

'Scotoma' (2009) in the Kunsthalle Bern was displayed as an appendix of the museum and, at the same time, as a surveillance mechanism that recorded the 'outside' of the museum and questioned the coherence of the translation of information between the framing archive of the museum and the reality.

> Architecture is a media. Cinema and a house alike transform perception while making a selection, and architecture is in this sense a technology. Like any other media, architecture shows how perception is constructed, how it can be manipulated, and how it can be developed and changed. Perception starts from the body and from its way of reacting to technology, it's the same with architecture. Language is also a way to construct/affect perception. An image with a sentence, for example, changes completely the image. But also language changes the image through the way you refer to an image. This is the way technology and media are appearing in my work.
>
> (Silva 2007 interview)

Fig. 4.1: Sancho Silva, Faro, 2008, Fábrica da Cerveja, Faro, ©Sancho Silva.

Michael Eng evaluates Silva's work in the perspective of the inheritance of modernity. In his article *Sancho Silva. Film Machine* (Eng 2003), he regards the relationship between architecture and cinema as an attempt to release architecture from its static condition. This architecture in movement is an architectonic space, in which time has been introduced as an architecture of the event. The relationship between architecture and optics is traced back by Eng to Walter Benjamin's essay 'The Work of Art in the Age of Mechanical Reproduction' (Benjamin 1936). Cinema is seen by Benjamin as providing access to an unconscious optics of space, similar to the access provided by psychoanalysis to the unconscious, at a time when both cinema and

Fig. 4.2-4.3: Sancho Silva, Fly in the Eye, 2008, Czech Republic, ©Sancho Silva.

psychoanalysis were taking shape, and the link between the birth of cinema and the birth of psychoanalysis started to be explored. While mapping this connection with key moments in 20th-century art, Eng brings Bernard Tschumi's deconstructive work with the cinematic metaphor into the discussion. As a continuation of the modernist project, cinema is an observant, trained subject that is postmodern, in the sense that it has the knowledge to assimilate a discontinuous image sequence. Another perspective that Micheal Eng brings to the work of Silva is that of Jonathan Crary (Crary 1996, 2002), who regards the viewer as an individual that can be conditioned in his reception, by the means of certain techniques of the body, to which he is forced to submit. An architectural construction conditions the observation of the subject and, while in modernity the observer is perceived as activating the building by his presence, the building in Silva's work activates the experience of the subject, which inverts for Eng the modern relationship. The five observation tubes in Silva's 'Film Machine' correspond to the five prison bars that block the view of the prisoner, and in this way, for Eng, the technology of observation is connected here with the role that architecture has played in the history of cinema.

As only the outer shell is visibly perceivable from any medial device – if it is architecture or a mechanical or a digital machine – the invisible part has always been the object of scrutiny and interpretation. Under the visibility of the medium, an invisible domain is always present that remains unknown. Boris Groys (2000) talks about the 'suspicious' sub-medial space, since the viewer always presumes that something is hidden 'under' it. Although there is a constant fascination for this unknown medial space, it cannot be mapped through a factual examination. The reason Groys sees in the fact that by a technical inspection the medium would lose its quality of medium and would become a usual object. This has the consequence that the viewer is constantly waiting for the medium to become the message. The sub-medial space that Groys compares to a cultural archive is maintained through a suspicion that is infinite because it cannot be satisfied. Still for Groys, this sub-medial space is not connected to the essence of a work, but is a space of subjectivity onto which the viewer projects his own personal suspicion. Groys sees the relationship between recipient and medium as based on subjectivity: based on his own suspicion, the subject produces the mediality of the other that cannot be other than subjective.

In Yukihiro Taguchi's 'The Last Chair'[1] (2008), looking through a camera on a tripod, which was placed in the gallery space facing a pile of wood dust, the audience could see a video in which this pile of wood became the chair, followed by its playback of the destruction of the chair back into the wood particles again. The video-camera is playing ironically on the idea of media as interface, being a false interface, one that does not transmit what takes place 'under its surface' and that does not connect the viewer with the reality 'behind the lens', but rather with a virtual presence of the chair in front of him, one that traverses different stages of its material presence in time. The work also alludes to digital–analogue crossings: the illusion of a chair being rebuilt through the medium of a digital camera is both undermined and complemented by the reality of the chair itself, which is presented as the 'proof' of the material consistency of the digital processes it has undergone.

The virtual real

The overlapping of the real and the virtual came into attention, starting with the appearance of a new digital object in which these two realities collide and coexist. The virtual is not seen as a new reality, but the real is understood from the perspective of its virtuality. In thinking about the virtual, Slavoj Žižek (1996: 290–295) recalls the psycho-analytical work of Jacques Lacan. Lacan discloses that the constitution of reality is based ultimately on fantasy, grounded in the assumption that the human awareness of reality is formed through the exclusion of a traumatic reality. Reality is constituted, in his view, through a detour into fantasy in order to repress another reality. Following this line of thought, Žižek relies on Freud's famous example of a father dreaming that his son is burning, in which the father awakes, unable to stand the dream-reality of his burning son. Here a change of register of conscience takes place, from the dream-state to being awake, which translates a jump from the impossible enduring of the reality of the dream to the liberating fantasy effect (or unreality effect) of the reality. Through this principle, Žižek also explains the digital reality of the virtual computer world, which he designates as an *evocative* object (Žižek 1996: 292). The simulation of human thinking through a computer is brought so close to the original that the situation shows its reverse side, and the question emerges as to whether human intelligence operates like a computer, and can be programmed by itself and understood as programmed. As the computer is based on a similarity with the reality, which must be excluded in order to be comprehensible with a computer, that which we designate as real is ultimately based on fantasy, as it is based on the same exclusion of that which we experience as a 'hard, external' reality, which we cannot include in our image of reality.

In this way the virtual brings its final lesson, according to Žižek's argument, through the observation that the virtual virtualizes reality: in the fascination with the virtual, so-called substantial reality is perceived as a copy of itself, as a pure symbolic construction: 'The fact that the computer does not think means that our price for our access to reality consists in the fact that something has to remain unthought'. (Žižek 1996: 295).

Žižek's perspective, repeated in different domains of thought in the last few decades, is detaching virtual reality from a technical dimension, which is related to concrete, quantifiable media equipment and conditions, and projecting it onto a philosophical dimension, which has various consequences that are embedded in the domain of art. Žižek's perspective opens an interpretation of the virtual that stresses the process of sliding from a real condition (in the sense of present, actual), to a condition of non-actuality (the no-less-real presence of an object in a dream). In this sense the virtual is connected to the conscience of an impossible perception of reality (unless it is virtualized). This is an insight that grounded the impact and expansion of computer-generated augmented reality.

Cyberspace and substituted real: Some theories of the virtual connected to the digital

Another strain of literature, on the virtual connected to the digital, understood the virtual as the effect of technique upon the senses, which determines apparitions that *seem* like reality. In these cases, the virtual appears as a fake reality. The possibility of interaction with this virtual domain is based on artificiality, telepresence and immersion for Michael Heim (1993). In his cult book, *The Metaphysics of Virtual Reality,* Heim regards digital reality as *art*, due to its power to transform our consciousness (Heim 1993: 124) and to detach 'the user' from the 'real' and concrete world.[2] Benjamin Wooley (1993), another theoretician of cyberspace, considers every virtual reality a *simulation* of an ideal computer, a universal machine/prototype, which is dispensing the human contribution to the 'realization' of the virtual. In his interpretation, the virtual is based on an *imitation* of reality and on a representation of human intelligence. Simulation is, therefore, the fiction of the digital era; a copy of something that has lost its origin (Wooley 1993: 247).[3]

The first theories of the virtual as a digitally-produced reality were dual and antagonistic concerning the relationship of real vs. virtual. Regarding the new access to the virtual brought by the digital world, Paul Virilio (Wilson 1996: 323) talks about a decomposed, ambivalent reality that has nothing to do with simulation, but with a problem of substitution. Relating to Jean Baudrillard, Virilio declares the idea of the simulation of 'real' reality through virtual reality to be already outdated. He suggests the focus should be rather on a *substitution* (through technical means) of *actual* reality through the virtual, which Virilio considers to be an *accident*. The two existing realities (the virtual and the actual) are connected in a symmetrical relationship with each other (Virilio 1996: 323): virtual reality is the cyberspace of technical proficiency, which is as real as what we used to call 'reality'. Virilio stresses that the two worlds are completely separate, which he terms the 'drama of the division of the human being' (Virilio 1996: 323). The moment in which virtual reality becomes stronger than actual reality is the moment of the big accident of humanity, which Virilio predicts, which has not yet been experienced. In this way, reality will stop being a subject for art, and will become the matter of art, and art will be made with it (Virilio 1996: 328).

The digital computer world also brought up another phenomenon that was extensively commented upon: the mistrust in the object, due to its artificiality. Vilem Flusser talks about the *digital apparition* (Flusser 1996: 242–245). The question that Flusser addresses is: are the alternative worlds as real as the 'real' world, or is the 'real' world as ghostlike as the alternative worlds? The difference, in Flusser's view, is the density of the bits and the pixels that constitute the digital. An object is as 'real' as bigger its density and as 'potential' (Flusser 1996: 244) as lower and dispersed its density. The real is, therefore, nothing more than an accumulation of as many realizations of potentialities as possible. Flusser is calling for the realization of worlds through the design of realities that the more dense they are, the more effective (Flusser 1996: 244).

Art, the event and actualizing the virtual

The theory of technology is developed further with regard to its power to actualize the virtual by Brian Massumi (1998: 16–24). For him, technology makes not only actualization possible, but also controls and manipulates the appearance of the virtual. Massumi also considers that in the contemporary world, art has the particular role of making possible different ways of actualization, due to its position on the borderline between the actual and the virtual. Massumi connects the power of art to actualize the virtual with the dimension of the event. In his text on art 'Sensing the Virtual, Building the Insensible' (1998: 16–24) he discusses the reality of the event as being the reality of the virtual. He explains that it is impossible for an actual form/presence to embody an event in a concrete way, since the event is based on the continuous transformation of its object. In this case, there is theoretically no possibility for the virtual to be created in an actual form. The virtual cannot be found in situations and objects, but solely in states of alteration – in other words in an object caught in a state of transformation.

> If the virtual is change as such, then in any actually given circumstance it can only figure as a mode of abstraction. For what is concretely given is what is – which is not what it will be when it changes. The potential of a situation exceeds its actuality. Circumstances self-abstract to the precise extent to which they evolve. This means that the virtual is not contained in any actual form assumed by things or states of things. It runs in the transitions from one form to another.
>
> (Massumi 1998: 16)

Brian Massumi shifts the focus from the domain of the virtual and the actual onto the process of actualization itself, and constructs a fine borderline – the frontier between virtual and actual – where, for him, the biggest potential of creative transformation can be found.

The virtual as a state of alteration that surpasses any actual form and that encompasses transformation and multiplicity stands at the core of the so-called post-digital understanding of the object. The object does not contain the virtual, but on the contrary, the virtual is its own state of natural, persisting metamorphosis. The object of the post-digital thinking fluctuates between imagined forms, digital algorithms and 3D printed shapes, in a perpetuating process, without attaining an end state. It is drawn from natural arrangements which are corroborated with digital diagrams, configuring a new objectual identity.

The term 'post-digital' was first introduced in Kim Cascone's 'The Aesthetics of Failure: Post-Digital Tendencies in Contemporary Computer Music' (Cascone, 2000), as cited by Ian Andrew (2002). As Andrew explains, in music the term post-digital designates works that started to reject the purity and perfection of digital sound in favour of errors, glitches, artefact and analogue sounds. On the other hand, post-digital is also a temporal determination, refering to the natural continuation of the trajectory of digital art. Associated to it were different strategies of understanding the object beyond the digital illusionistic composition, for example by the rejection of

Fig. 4.4: Sinta Werner, 4xDoublefixed / Classic Aluminium, 2009, Kunstverein Aichach, ©Sinta Werner.

Fig. 4.5: Sancho Silva, Faro, 2008, Fábrica da Cerveja, Faro, ©Sancho Silva.

combination media strategies (re-use, appropriation, re-presentation, cut-up) and pure digital frabrication. Lev Manovich (2002), for example, advocates for a new aesthetic that should come closer to modernism in the first step. Nevertheless the idea of digital progress is implicitly negated by the term, and formulates thereof an aesthetic position. In recent design and art the term designates a shift from the preoccupation with optimizing technology to its role in a multistratified object between natural, biological and programmed innnovation and mutation.

The virtual, as it emerges in this post-digital object, can be understood as a result of lowtech assemblages, biotech rythms (like bone or plant growth), microscopic structures and the movements of tectonic configurations (like water flow or earth structures) and most recent techniques of introducing subtle 'genetic' changes in natural algorythms. As a recent exhibition in the Museum of Arts and Design in New York (2014) implies[4] critical, self reflexive notes traverse these experiments regarding the borders of digital and analogue creation: for example as revealed by Hiroshi Sugimoto's attempt to find the meaning of Japanese mathematical models manufactured in the 19th century, by recasting them as aluminium digital sculptures (2006).

The post-digital does not aim to describe a life *after* digital, but an object that can assume any technological form and is permanently responsive to its context. The post-digital is marked also by a new importance given to autonomous systems, that are generated by the artists or by machines but which take an unpredictable course, either in human interaction or in computer algorythms. The object is therefor physically fabricated as the set for a multiaxial performance, subjected to constant interference. Finally, the digital machine turns, without human intervention, organic, subverting the logic of production. A post-digital architecture can be in this sense thought of as responsive, non-prescriptive solution and intervention.

The event as phenomenon of emergence of the virtual: At Deleuze

At the core of this short overview of definitions of the virtual stands the vision of Gilles Deleuze on the role of the performative event for the formation of the virtual. In his book *The Fold. Leibniz and the Baroque*, and especially in the chapter 'What is an event', Deleuze is differentiating between the two understandings of an event in the writings of Gottfried Wilhelm Leibniz and Alfred North Whitehead (Deleuze 2006b).
Alfred North Whitehead, a thinker of modernity, whose philosophy is strongly connected to the thinking of Albert Einstein, is presented by Deleuze as a thinker of duration. His vision

stands for the modern world with its divergences, oppositions and incompatibilities, and contrary to the baroque diversity of possible worlds, represented through the philosophy of Leibniz. In that which Deleuze shows as being specifically modern in the figure of Whitehead lies the essence of what Deleuze himself considers to be the functioning principles of the event. Leibniz is understood by Deleuze as a thinker who connects the event with the possible, the event being a result of the possible. Deleuze therefore approaches the event following Whitehead's line of thought and sees the event as a *temporary densification of potentialities.*

For Deleuze, an event results from a set of specific forces and means together with other events that take place at the same time. It is a unique moment of change in a flux of changes that take place in the cosmos. Each of these events has kept its certain specificity, during its production.

In the chapter 'What is an event' (Deleuze 2006b: 86–95), Deleuze enumerates the conditions of the event: extension, intensity, the individual and *prehensions,*[5] while following Whitehead's theory of the event stating that events stand in an extensive relationship to each other. Events as transitive phenomena are parts of other events. The event is a part of an infinite series of events connected to each other. For Deleuze, an event gets actualized in facts, in space and time, and acquires thereby concrete data and also symbolic value, but in itself an event is determined by another spatiality and temporality and by a condensation of that which Deleuze calls the *incompossibilities.* This is how Whitehead expresses a detachment from the Baroque thought of Leibniz:

> For Leibniz, as we have seen, bifurcations and divergences of series are genuine borders between incompossible worlds, such that the monads[6] that exist wholly include the compossible world that moves into existence. For Whitehead (and for many modern philosophers), on the contrary, bifurcations, divergences, incompossibilities, and discord belong to the same motley world [...] In a same chaotic world divergent series are endlessly tracing bifurcating paths. It is a 'chaosmos' [...].
>
> (Deleuze 2006b: 91)

Deleuze regards the *Chaosmos* that he derives from Whitehead as a space of modernity. The event is connected to place and non-place, with action and non-action, with plurality, which is due to a condensation of *virtual possibilities.*

> With the neo-Baroque, with its unfurling of divergent series in the same world, comes the irruption of incompossibilities on the same stage, where Sextus will rape *and* not rape Lucretia, where Caesar crosses *and* does not cross the Rubicon, where Fang kills, is killed, and neither kills nor is killed. In its turn harmony goes through a crisis that leads to a broadened chromatic scale, to emancipation of dissonance or of unresolved accords, accords not brought back to a tonality.
>
> (Deleuze 2006b: 91)

The event can be positively and negatively assessed at the same time, and places itself between what exists and does not exist, between true and false. In this way, real or imaginary, imagined or already occurred, are not fixed terms and remain undecided as the event itself is escaping a definition. In this way, the event is connected by Deleuze with the problem of becoming and the problem of repetition. Deleuze understands the event as potentiality and as virtuality. This 'event as virtuality' happens in the moments that Deleuze describes as the hesitation of the world before a happening, before its actualization in time and space. He understands the event as the expectation of an event in-between many co-existent oppositions.[7]

> An event does not just mean that a man has been run over. […] Events are produced in a chaos, in a chaotic multiplicity, but only under the condition that a sort of screen intervenes. Chaos does not exist; it is an abstraction because it is inseparable from a screen that makes something – something rather than nothing – emerge from it.
>
> (Deleuze 2006b: 86)

The object is conceived by Deleuze not as a singular element, but as a *prehension* that can be understood only through that which has preceded and that which has succeeded it. It is an absorption of an entire world in an element. The event emerges through a movement of the world towards the subject, a movement that can have both a private and a public dimension, while the *new* emerges in the interaction between constant objectivization of a *prehension,* and the concomitant subjectivization of another. Events also have inherent qualities, and their intensities are part of other series in a process that, in this way, propagates more and more. Individuality is another component of the event for Deleuze. In this sense he follows Whitehead's understanding of individuality as the power of the event to produce something new. Through individuality the new is formed. Its significance is creativity, which is a personal state (Deleuze 2006b: 89).

In Difference and Repetition (Deleuze 1994), Deleuze explicitly stresses the fact that there is not a single way to think about virtuality, but there are many types of repetition, and each has its own way of calling forth another virtuality. The actualization of the virtual is therefore not a realization of something preformed.[8] Based on the assumption of the infinite differentiation of virtuality, actualization means an infinite differentiation, which means, for Deleuze, making space for the new, and the articulation of the future (Ott 2007).[9]

The possible and the illusionary space

Exploring the area of the illusion, until it achieves a physical, concrete presence, Sinta Werner's work can be approached by considering the distinction between the virtual and the possible, in other words the distinction between the real and the illusion. Deleuze repeatedly affirms across his writing, as quoted above, that the possible is *realized* through resemblance and limitation, whereas the virtual is *actualized* through difference and creation.

The possible has no reality. Contrary to that, the virtual has reality, even if it is not actualized. The possible is therefore a possibility of the real that precedes the real. The possible has no actuality, but it is similar to the reality, and it is limited by the reality and by the possibilities of the real (something is possible that can become real). The possible belongs therefore to the domain of the illusion: the possible can be true only if it can be possible. In this sense, the possible is throwing a new light on the question of the *new*. While the virtual is connected with the appearance of the new and the dimension of creation, the possible is connected to an apparent new, since it seems to produce the new, but actually produces only an illusion of the new.

Working with illusion, Sinta Werner rather explores the domain of the possible than that of the virtual, since her works consist mostly of reflections of spaces, which she constructs in heavy materials, extending the initial space and actually physically reproducing a mirrored reproduction of an already existing space. She is transforming an optical illusion (an unreal, but possible space) into matter. The initial spaces are doubled and their structuring axes are outstretched into the unreal. For example, in her work 'The Subversive Space'/'Der Subversive Raum' (2009), it becomes unclear whether the viewer is watching an unreal space that has been materialized, or the illusion of a material space. In her work, architecture is a media of representation that produces illusion. Werner works with collage photography, paintings, objects, installations and drawings, always oscillating between bi-dimensionality and the tri-dimensional. The distortions that she produces unmask their own artifices. The intention, therefore, seems to be less the *production* of an illusion and more the exploration of the territory, where the border of representation can be traversed and a crossing point between materiality and the non-material can be physically realized.

Mimesis versus simulation

The concept of mimesis, to which her work seems to stand very close, does not only connote the process of copying, but also implies the capacity of the object to transform and vary its qualities. There is a fine borderline between the object of 'mimesis' and the 'simulacrum', and this relationship reflects the difference between the domain of illusion and that of the virtual, which will come into attention in the following pages.

As the work of Sinta Werner can be brought closer to the domain of the possible than to that of the virtual (presenting an illusion of reality), her work also stands closer to being an act

Fig. 4.6: Sinta Werner, Dissolve, 2008, Model, Stedefreund, Berlin, ©Sinta Werner.

Fig. 4.7-4.8: Sinta Werner, Overshadowed,
2012, Photograph, ©Sinta Werner.

Fig. 4.9: Sinta Werner, Disjunction, 2007,
Installation view, Goldsmith's College,
London, ©Sinta Werner.

Fig. 4.10: Sinta Werner, Out of Frame, 2009, Installation view, Christinger de Mayo, Zürich, ©Sinta Werner.

of 'mimesis' (of reality), rather than being a 'simulacrum' of reality, which, as will be shown below in relation to the work of Carlos Bunga, is blended with the virtual.

Still, mimesis is not a simple copy of reality. In his text dedicated to *mimesis* Wolfgang Iser (1998: 670–668) explains that the discourse of mimesis is not only descriptive (mimesis does not only re-present or re-narrate its object) but it also justifies and legitimizes the act of emulation. The necessity of self-legitimization is identified and commented upon by Iser along the history of the mimesis tradition. Iser suggests that the transformation of an object can be achieved through explaining this object, based on a connection between the object, the discourse and the environment in which the discourse takes place. Through this transformation, which he designates as *emergence*, the performative dimension of *mimesis* is brought to the surface. Iser also talks about the simulacrum, which annuls objecthood and makes it volatile. The simulacrum is, for Iser, a representation of something non-existent, whereas mimesis always keeps its reference to an object. He sees the simulacrum as an heir of mimesis (Iser 1998: 676).

From this perspective, Sinta Werner's preoccupation with the performative use of illusion, and her way of constructing reality, can be connected to the idea of mimesis. The reference to the object, which Iser introduces in connection with mimesis, is a definite aspect of Sinta Werner's work. It is precisely the material dimension of the object that produces the illusion in Werner's work.

On the contrary, most of the works described here can be seen as being closer to the concept of simulacrum. Iser explains that the incorporeal character which the simulacrum confers to objecthood opens up an empty place, which can be occupied by the imaginary, whereas the product of this imagination can be infinitely variable. The performative dimension of discourse is a result of this dimension of the imagination (Iser 1998: 677).

The simulacrum as experience of the virtual

Following Carlos Bunga's definition of the term simulacrum, which he introduced to describe his process of creation, simulacrum represents an innovative object, which results from an alteration of reality and develops an unpredictable course of action from its object of reference (Bunga 2010 interview). This understanding of simulacrum does not view simulation as an imitation or copying of reality, but as a shift, a modification of the existing reality.

The idea of the copy without a model is relevant for works like Carlos Bunga's 'Corner' and 'Pillar' (2006) at the Art Fair Miami Beach, where what the viewer saw was the presence of an absence, a virtual corner or a virtual pillar, that, as the title suggests, is there, but there in

Fig. 4.11: Carlos Bunga, Ágora, 2012, Museu de Arte Contemporânea de Serralves, Porto, Photo, ©Filipe Braga, ©Fundação de Serralves, Porto, ©Carlos Bunga.

Fig. 4.12: Carlos Bunga, Ágora, 2012, Museu de Arte Contemporânea de Serralves, Porto, Photo, ©Filipe Braga, ©Fundação de Serralves, Porto, ©Carlos Bunga.

another time, and invisible in the present. What remain visible are the foundations or ruins of a pillar, and a corner that reproduces a corner, but at the same time the proportions of the initial architectural structure are changed. The 'pillar' and 'corner' are not present and not virtual, but stage an actualization of their virtual presence.

Architectural models are also objects that work on the level of the virtual. Returning to Carlos Bunga's 'Espacio Metaforico' (2010), the work that was discussed in the introduction of this volume, it becomes conspicuous that this model does not *anticipate* in miniature a construction, but loses its object of reference, as a simulacrum does. These objects can be regarded as *regressive prototypes* that go back in time (and are not oriented to the future, as models are), revealing hidden layers, similar to a ruin. Bunga's building technique is based on eliminating layers of matter that make visible other layers from beneath; a temporal process in which time is spun backwards and releases new configurations of matter and states of visibility. The qualities of a simulacrum are reinforced in his work also by the consistency of cardboard – the basic material of his work. It emulates durable materials and assumes their functions, but it is at the same time ephemeral. It is this ambivalence that has also opened up new possibilities in the area of construction and transportation industry to which Bunga also refers.

Carlos Bunga transposes this concept of the simulacrum from the material to his entire work. He defines the term as a model that shifts the function of the original and breaks with its referent (Bunga 2010 interview) and in this sense his apprehension resonates with Iser's theory. For Bunga, simulacrum is not a simulation, a copy, but nor does it belong to the domain of the imaginary, rather it belongs to that of the idea. It is what he calls a *potential*. Like Bunga, Michael Krome (2009 interview) also discusses the capacity of the simulacrum to realize a variation in relation to reality, and stresses the ambiguity of the correspondence between the simulacrum and its referent.

We can recall here also the complex connotations that the Middle Ages conferred upon the simulacrum, and the fear that surrounded it as an object of sophisticated ambiguity. Michael Camille (1966:31-44), a theoretician of the Middle Ages, writes that the notion of the simulacrum played its most important role in medieval culture, by the fact that it endangered the concept of representation itself and undermined the dichotomy between the divine model and the human made copy, between image and resemblance. Contrary to the mimetic image, which had been saluted as an affirmation of the real, the simulacrum was feared in the Middle Ages, as a negation of the real. Due to the fact that it was an image without a model, it disturbs the usual order of priority.[10] Camille expounds that the specific imitation realized by the simulacrum has to be referred back to Plato, for whom the simulacrum is a deviation and a perversion of imitation, a fake imitation. Moreover, the simulacrum for Plato seems true to its model only by viewing it from a certain perspective, which lets it *seem* something else. In this equation, human subjectivity is, therefore, of key importance. The simulacrum accordingly includes (from its beginnings as an important philosophical concept) not only the creator of image, but also the viewer (Camille 1996: 32).

Camille considers that Deleuze, in his understanding of the simulacrum, is reversing Plato, as he is renouncing the dualism of the Platonic interpretation. Especially in his book on the work of Francis Bacon *Logic of the Senses* (Deleuze 2005), and in the chapter 'The simulacrum and ancient philosophy' (Deleuze 2005: 291–303), the simulacrum is acknowledged by Deleuze as a fundamental concept for the art of our times. Deleuze replaces the Platonic precedence of the model over the copy using a reversed system, in which the simulacrum does not have to justify itself, and the dichotomous Platonic relationship is completely dissolved. Deleuze also renounces the perspective of the viewer, which defined the nature of the simulacrum in Plato (Camille 1996: 33).[11]

The term simulacrum also plays an important role in the work of Derrida. Simulation for him is connected to a performative manifestation, but in relation to his term *difference*[12].

Fig. 4.13: Hironari Kubota, A Man in the Sea of Japan, 2005, ©Hironari Kubota.

Fig. 4.14: Hironari Kubota, Heroes of Tragedy, 1997, ©Hironari Kubota.

Simulacrum is, in this case, the emergence of meaning in the course of repetition in a game between presence and absence, manifestation and disappearance, where the simulacrum maintains the dual nature of the two perspectives. For Derrida, the simulacrum is the means through which the *différance* between form and non-form is established as a mediation. It can be therefore deduced that through its relationship to *différance,* the simulacrum is strongly related to interaction and mediation.

Hironari Kubota creates in his spinning sessions a 'simulacrum' of another performative event, the Japanese Onbashira Festival, where heavy tree trunks are cut up in a complex Shinto ceremony and ridden down forest slopes by the participants in order to be transported to the shrine. In making reference to it, Kubota is emulating the 7th-century festival held until this day, once every six years, in the region of Nagano, but transposing it into another register in his performances, where he spins the heavy cars, the boat ('The Giant Spin of Fishing Boat in Kitakyushu', 2011) or the idol ('The Spinning Idol Senjyu-Kannon', 2011). It is the essence of this festival that Kubota intends to simulate: its force and its dramatic content that are restaged by the audience. But for Kubota, as he explains (Kubota 2011 interview), this is as well a critical and even cynical endeavour, and his mix of referents reloads the object of worship not only devotionally but analytically as well. His simulacrum spinning object has here a ritualistic content, in the sense of a re-enactment of a spiritual nature that both copies and deviates from a certain 'order'. This reflected and recreated simulacrum, similar to the one mentioned by M. Camille in reference to the medieval idol, is both reinforcing, delineating and examining his object. Danger, devotion, amazement and fear are the forces that Kubota extracts from his experience of Onbashira, and infuses his own performances consequently with this undetermined potential. This unruly force of nature is a dimension that Kubota himself does not completely control in his pieces:

> My work is also built around this principle: it is very simple and once my installation starts to work,[13] to function, even I cannot stop it myself, it works with the power of its own speed and so, every time I have a performance, I am afraid. The material is very heavy and, also, I cannot control this movement of my installation; but the construction is solid so, on the other hand, that makes it safe. This fear – for the people and mine, too – and the fact that I cannot control these elements is for me also connected to this festival. […] I am not mainly interested in nature itself in my work. For me the city is also nature. The car I use in my installations is a tool for me, which can change its nature, it can be many things at the same time, and it can become suddenly something else. I use objects in ways that make them change shape, change expression until people do not recognize them anymore; until it is not possible to decide any more if this is a car or if it is a stone. This is what is interesting to me.
>
> (Kubota 2011 interview)

As will be seen in the interview on page 186, the 30 minutes of spinning the ready-made sculptures of Hironari Kubota affirm the familiar presence of a quotidian (but at the same time ritual) object and also give access into its virtual identity, a metaphysical register of meaning, recalling the fact that, for Gilles Deleuze, the event is both real and unreal, has already, and not yet, occurred. For Gilles Deleuze the event means an actualization of potentialities, while being connected to an essential duality that he calls unresolved accords (Deleuze 2006b: 91). The status and the nature of the 'simulacrum' object with which Kubota works remains ambiguous, caught between multiple medial manifestations that are both happening and not. In the discourse of Kubota (Kubota 2011 interview), simulation or the simulacrum-object is highly nuanced. The idea of representation, which is an inherent part of it, recalls for him the domain of visuality. While affirming that his work is not exactly a destruction of form, but 'It is rather a change. I destroy *an image*' (Kubota 2011 interview), he alludes to the power to negate the real, to undermine the relationship of original-copy and by destroying an image, to destroy not only an appearance, but the *essence* of the reproduced object. As he explains in the interview on page 133–134, this is the reason for which he prefers to change the material of the original cult statue of Senju-Kannon into styrofoam. In this shift the statue ceases to be itself and becoms a representation. The role of the audience in this transformatory process, in which the simulacrum of the statue becomes a tool of critical thinking and personal reassessment, is essential. In this sense, the power of the simulacrum turns to be strongly related to interaction and mediation. It is not the creator of the image (the artist), that can be considered the author of this simulacrum, but moreover the viewer which makes the shift of signigficance possible and goes himself through a transformation by watching the Kannon spin.

The concept of the simulacrum is reflected in the way Kubota depicts his own act of creation: 'For me, art is a way to change the material, the matter, and I also use my own body for this, since otherwise I cannot express my mind and show this interior image. In this process, movement receives almost material qualities; it is a concrete component of my work' (Kubota 2011). •

Interviews

Interview with Carlos Bunga, March 2010[14]

Q: Can you talk, please, about the idea of simulacrum, and your critical use of it?

C.B.: Simulacrum is, for me, not so much a copy in a formalist way, but near to the concept of a model. When I made my first small models, the first one came very close to reality. The point is to make use of a certain reality, but to use it in a more abstract way, to change its content. The simulacrum creates a shift: it could be reality, but it is not exactly reality. I think Matta Clark works much more than me on the quality of realness of the houses, with their social identity and life story, in a certain context – this is his working material. That is why he also works inside the already built houses. As for me, I am more interested in constructing an idea of a building and then destroying it. I am interested in the shift of layers of representation that the idea of simulacrum brings, of the transformation from something into another, on the basis of a formal logical system. The simulacrum, like a model, seems to be something concrete, but it is not. Instead I consider it rather as a projection of a space. It is one idea, one possible idea, rather than a concrete idea: it is a projection. This is where its critical potential lies. Also my use of cardboard and tape, such unstable materials, brings my action of constructing and deconstructing into the arena of simulacrum. I am performing a simulacrum of destruction, therefore of action, when collapsing my installations.

Q: By adding another layer of material and creating this simulacrum of space, departing from a white cube gallery or an institutional edifice like a bank, your transformation of these politically connoted spaces has an anarchic potential. How far do you go with the polemic of the simulacrum in the direction of institutional critique?

C.B.: My work makes an institutional critique, in the sense that what I am trying to do is create new possibilities for a space (that is why I build a simulacrum of that space). I would like to bring to people's attention the fact that virtually every space could have other connotations. Of course, the possibility of suggesting for a bank that it be defined through the provisional, fragile material of cardboard makes a social statement. This is one direction in which my work leads, but it originates not only in my intention to practise institutional critique, but also in various preoccupations with space that I follow. I always keep the name of the work attached to the name of the original space: 'Milton Keynes project', 'Elba Benitez project' etc. They remain very open. If I only alluded to

Fig. 4.15-4.17: Carlos Bunga, Ruins Project, 2009, ©Carlos Bunga.

Fig. 4.18: Carlos Bunga, Gran Esfera, 2010, Cardboard, paint and wood on Carrara marble pedestal, Carrara, Italy, ©Carlos Bunga.

Fig. 4.19: Carlos Bunga, Planos verticales entrecruzados, 2010, Cardboard, paint and wood on Carrara marble pedestal, Carrara, Italy, ©Carlos Bunga.

banks, as in the 'Culturgeste project', for example, it would really limit the reception by the audience.

In my present 'Art Unlimited Basel project' (2008), I have chosen the title 'Ruins', which makes the intentionality more specific, of course. We will have a publication on ruins from different scholarly perspectives, and I will make some 'documentary' drawings that alter my own installation in Basel. 'Unlimited' goes together with 'Art Basel' and it is supposed to be something monumental. And in response, I wanted to do something which is not expected of me so much, such as the monumentality of my previous installations and the monumentality of an art fair, but something more discrete, something non-monumental. For me, ruins are a space for thinking, especially in the context of an art fair.

Q: What role does virtuality play in the economy of your work, and why? What is the virtual for you?

C.B.: The economy of the means that I use in my work is profoundly related to the realization of works using different tools. We are surrounded by daily objects and stimuli with a great symbolic charge, and criteria such as permanency, stability, solidity are very important. What I am interested in is the possibility of multifaceted thinking about a universe which is constituted by objects that can have more open and ambiguous meanings. The variation of ideas and forms that my works provoke is meant to allow a greater flexibility in the manner of understanding the world.

Virtuality implies the idea of simulacrum for me, starting from a real referent that suffered an intervention, and remaining in the domain of the potential. In my work, virtuality is connected with experimentation with ever-present erosion and entropy and their causes and effects. Virtuality is also connected to a permanent consciousness of the vulnerability of objects.

Q: You are working with documentation, with scrutinizing past forms from the perspective of the present, renovating them constantly. What is the connection between virtuality and the new, as an outcome of art, in your opinion?

C.B.: Virtuality emerges as a necessity regarding the relation between real/unreal: it can eliminate the frontier that exists between both of them. The connection with the new can be made through the intermediary spaces, which exist between things, and that enhance the possibility of emergence of thought and experimentation.

Q: Your works are site-specific. Are you interested in the implementation of your work in a certain environment, in the historical and social environment in which it is exhibited? Or are you interested, rather, in showing certain mechanisms in an abstract way?

C.B.: My works are made from different media, taking elements from the environment as well as from the history of places and their social implications. Many of my works are created starting with a real referent, but are shown in a way that can contain different levels of abstraction. My work is strongly connected to the ideas of absence and emptiness or material leftovers, which enhance other notions, such as the force of suggestion and potentiality.

This manner of understanding the objects allows space for questioning. They are open works, which provide the possibility of a more flexible understanding of the way of thinking about and relating to the objects. The abstract mechanisms raise uncertainties, since they lack concreteness in regard to particular cases. Our thinking is structured between codes, categorizations or ideologies in the mental processes of grasping our surroundings.

We inherit a tradition of thinking in the way we relate to the world. And so there exists a need for constant renovation and transformation in the way we adapt to and understand the ecosystem.

Q: In the way you explain it, your work is not concerned with demolition and destruction in itself, but mostly with their staging and provocation, as in a laboratory. You said in another interview, it is about their simulation. Do you collect your postcards and newspapers as the real events? Are you interested in their belonging to reality and describing a state of 'post' the event, with its entire catastrophic atmosphere, contrary to the simulations in your work? Or, on the contrary, do you also consider them, like your works, as a representation of decay in time, filtered through a medium? So are you interested in their mediality, or in their content/realness?

C.B.: The demolition and destruction of the objects is part of the process of understanding the world around us. Demolition and destruction relate to a work, which develops through experimentation in a laboratory, where there constantly exists some staging of these open processes.

This processual laboratory induces us into the study of real referents in an unreal space, where actions take place in the virtuality of the two states of demolition and construction.

A simulacrum gives the possibility of projecting these codes of the real world into the work process, in an attempt to understand or make visible components, situations or reactions which have previously not been activated, or which pass by without being perceived.

Fig. 4.20: Carlos Bunga, Simultaneo, Fragmentado, Decontinuo, 2010, 29th Sao Paulo Biennial, ©Carlos Bunga.

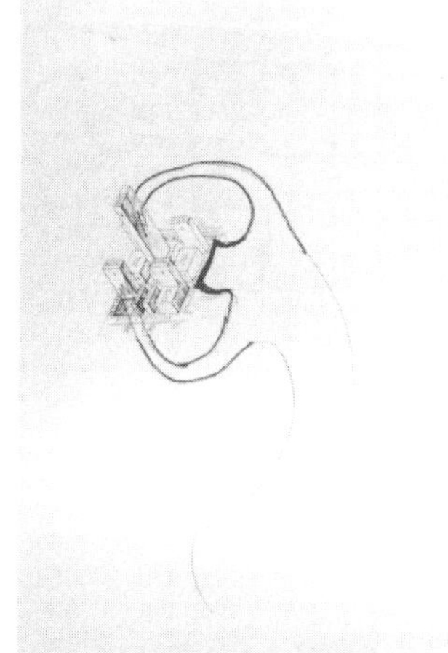

Fig. 4.21: Carlos Bunga, Nomada VII, 2008, Ink and collage on paper, ©Carlos Bunga.

Fig. 4.22: Carlos Bunga, Mutations I
(Intervention on reproduction of Frank
Lloyd Write's Lake Tahoe Summer Colony
1923), 2008, ©Carlos Bunga.

Fig. 4.23: Carlos Bunga, Mutations IV (Intervention on reproduction of Frank Lloyd Write's Bouweries Tower Project, 1927/31), 2008, ©Carlos Bunga.

Fig. 4.24: Carlos Bunga, Ausence, 2010, Exhibition view, Cardboard, paint and wood on Carrara marble pedestal, Carrara, Italy, ©Carlos Bunga.

Fig. 4.25: Carlos Bunga, House Plan, 2010, Cardboard, paint and wood on Carrara marble pedestal, Carrara, Italy, ©Carlos Bunga.

It is necessary that objects or documents, like post-cards, journals or real historic facts, exist, which can be brought into the laboratory, understood as a mental space, and processed in this intermediary space of personal or collective experience. Between the two, the real space and the mental laboratory, a constant process of meaning exchange takes place, where the objects and documents are involved in an active way. These documents, newspapers and objects are part of the past, of history, and function as artefacts, or as fragments, in a state of decomposition.

The objects are themselves a space in constant transformation and subjected to questionings, so that there is no finalized form in their structure. Any finalized form induces a meaning of death and, as a consequence, the process of its restoration comes out as a necessity of perpetuating the form through its memory of time. Great catastrophes accelerate the temporality of the objects and this is strongly related with this performative side present in many of my realized works.

Either in a physical dimension, or regarding small quotidian gestures, temporal acceleration is present on various levels of time and space. Decay is permanently active in any medium, which is developing in time, and is strictly related with the idea of death. Nevertheless, it brings a cyclical notion of the processes in which things are caught, and brings a direction of time involved in constant processes of transformation and rebirth.

Q: Which is the specificity of your approach to documentation of a disaster, in relation to other forms of collecting evidence, such as in journals, postcards etc.?

C.B.: The documentation in general is related with the virtual because they both are based on records that belong to the past and help us understand the future. This virtuality of the record of historical events in the work that I develop is for me a constant presence. Between the past (documentation) and the future (virtuality) there is this mutual reflection: the experience of the present; the laboratory space.

In this intermediary of the temporality of every process, which develops in a cyclical movement, the different eras of history interconnect. Therefore, in my laboratory I try to demonstrate the possibility of transforming ecosystems because we can add, subtract, multiply, correct, restore or accelerate.

Q: Human actions seem to occupy a backstage position in your work. Humans have an agency but remain unseen: for instance you build and deconstruct, but the audience doesn't feel your presence. You often work on human habitation sites, which imply a lived experience, on urban environments or on other constructions, which are all an outcome of human creation processes, but humans and their activities do not seem to leave their traces. Why do you feel the necessity of showing situations according to their unrepresentable side, rather than 'documenting' their visible side?

C.B.: There has always been this tendency and a consciousness about trying not to represent. So representation was constructed in art by showing a referent of reality fragmenting its representation and transmitting its meaning in a more conceptual or abstract way. This manner of showing things is more open to different readings, which makes it possible to vary models of thought and understanding. These reflections hold implicitly the referent of reality, but are shown in my work as fragments of a much more complex structure, which is not experienceable in real time. Since the concepts encompass a dimension, different from the one in which the objects are situated, the objects can become a pretext of dialogue in time with many interrelated concepts. The unrepresentable can raise abstract questions about reality, and can raise questions about practices of categorizing objects, and about their permanency. The unrepresentable can have not only objects as a referent, but also the domain of thought.

Q: The virtual is now connected so much to digital media, but you construct virtuality with completely different means. Where does the specificity of your modality of operating with the virtual lie?

C.B.: The virtual is *concretely* connected to digital media in relation to the time/space that we know and in which we live. Technology is an integral part of a society where something always ends up missing, and where the existence of objects is also related to the appropriation of images as an exercise of a constant approximation of reality by technology. Artificiality emerges from these relations: reality is like a screen projection – a new reality that came through technology.

Virtuality is present in the overall processes of my work and is present also in the material that I use, which is characteristic of my working process: cardboard. Cardboard is an industrial object, resulting from a society of consumption, of mass culture, of trends, of emigration, of different languages and perceptions, and carries with it the social and political function of 'the world in the era of technical reproducibility'. What I make visible in my work is a transformation of experience that relates to the degradation or to the ephemeral side of a construction. This process of degradation of the ephemeral, which belongs to a virtual dimension, is also connected to a temporal dimension of the *instant* experience.

I use cardboard, but I do not speak about cardboard. Cardboard functions as a medium for reflecting languages that have, as a background, the referent time/space or real/unreal.

Interview with Sinta Werner, July 2009

Q: Let's start by talking about the way you construct space by reflection of its material components.

S.W.: My approach is very clear in a work like 'The Subversive Space' (2009). This work is a reflection of the entire ceiling and another corner of the space that was distorted so the copied space permeates the original

Fig. 4.26: Sinta Werner, Disjunction, 2007, Installation view, Goldsmith's College, London, ©Sinta Werner.

space without completely coinciding. What has interested me here is the fragmentation of the space, as if it was a cubistic, three-dimensional installation.

Q: You mean a unification of various perspectives in the same plane?

S.W.: That is right. The forms are interlaced in a cubist manner and the viewer loses orientation.

Q.: Are you working with models or with a computer program?

S.W There is a professional program for that, but I work with models directly on the site, with an assistant, and having as a starting point the ground plan that I have transformed into a model. In another work, '4 x Doublefixed / Classical Aluminium' (2009), I have constructed an imaginary reflection, whereas the theatricality comes from the impression of a not yet mounted exhibition. The effect is total, since all the details are doubled, but the viewer is stricken by the missing of his own reflection. In a group show in Stedefreund Gallery, Berlin, 2009 I created a work with Markus Wüste, where we took samples from the architecture of the inside space of the gallery and inserted them again as objects of display into the gallery space. They seemed to be objects from another environment projected into the space. In a similar procedure we have taken a fragment of an apartment door that we simply twisted and inserted back into the door, which produced an estrangement effect, although the fragment belonged originally to that same context. It's interesting that the viewer is tempted to correct optically the twisted part, and therefore the whole space seems contorted and starts to oscillate.

Q: Please talk about your use of material in building up a relation between reality and illusion. Your work has an intense material presence. You work with heavy installations, but on the other hand this materiality is paradoxically what brings the image into a domain of projection of an immaterial illusion. Do you always work with original material used in construction or is the heavy materiality also illusionary?

S.W.: In some works I use the original material, since I am more interested in a sculptural quality. In others I am more interested in the image in space. I have worked in this sense also with photography as a tri-dimensional medium, where I have prolonged the architectural perspectives of the buildings photographed, by folding the photography itself. I have always been interested in realizing spatiality through painting, using illusion as well in the opposite direction, flattening space through painting. It is important for me to rupture the borders between image, sculpture, space so that they converge.

Fig. 4.27: Sinta Werner, Versionen, 2009, Installation view: Appartement 'Versionen', Berlin, ©Sinta Werner.

Fig. 4.28-4.29: Sinta Werner, Der schizophrene Raum, 2010, Domaquaree, Berlin, ©Sinta Werner.

Q: How important is the concept of illusion for you? While you are making an illusion of illusion (an illusion of a mirror), is it for you its negation, a way of surpassing illusion, or are you interested rather in a reinforced illusion, a utopic environment?

S.W.: I am thinking rather about questions like: 'What are you doing if you do not see your image in the mirror?' I would like to leave this space undefined: the mirror is a space that brings the viewer into another place, but it makes you also conscious about a here and now. The point of departure for me is having some rules: manipulating them and creating something non-logical, until these rules do not function any more. I want to work with these rules in order to create something irrational.

Q: You construct illusionary spaces in different media: the tri-dimensional installations that are perceived as mirrored images, your minimal paintings that are graphically flattened, the photographic collages and the folded photographs that turn the bi-dimensional medium of photography into a sculptural object. Is illusion for you a means to pass from one of these forms/dimensions of visuality and of representation, into another?

S.W.: Mainly, I am trying to thematize the state in between image and space, to provoke a dematerialization that picks up on the tradition of abstract, plain, minimal painting.

Q: What is your relation to the objects, since your illusion of space results from concrete materiality?

S.W.: Canvas is also a material presence, it's a support. In this sense it is at the same time an abstracted space.

Q: How do you perceive your position as a manipulator of experience? What are the effects that you expect?

S.W.: I am not interested in my position in these processes, but rather in a short moment of control, which each of the viewers might be forced to leave, and with it also leave the domain of the illusion. The works are a metaphor for the fact that our common experience of architecture is very limited. I am trying to suggest a point of view that would fragment and break its continuity in space. I am thinking about a quote of Claire Bishop, in her book *Installation Art* (Bishop 2001), commenting on the fact that nowadays installation art reflects a decentred subject and also a fragmented space. In these illusionary spaces we can analyse, therefore, a social condition.

Q: What are the principles according to which you abstract reality?

S.W.: The principle is an interplay between frontstage and backstage. The stage is not a real space; it is just a façade that reproduces 'reality'. In my work the scaffold has an equal importance like the building and its aesthetic interests me especially. It is functional.

Q: Where do these concomitant directions in your work lead: production (illusion) and reduction (structure, abstractization)?

S.W.:   This relation has to do for me with the mathematical coordinates in which we live, but is also about the artificiality of the built space. In Greece I have started to work with landscape: I have recorded stone formations and created through collage cloned landscapes with impossible perspectives.

Q: Do you work with a disjunction between space and time? Is there a temporal continuum with the initial spaces, or do you create time rupture like your cracks within space?

S.W.:   I am working rather with a freezing of time, which happens in the short moment of illusion. In the 'Subversive Space' I had the impression that architecture was slowly sinking and was solidified in this movement.

Q: Do you work with principles of architectural construction that you apply to various media (like collage, photography) or do you rather manipulate these principles in order to show a dysfunctionality and split representation?

S.W.:   Space in my works is rather dysfunctional, and occupied with something that cannot be used. It becomes an object of art, and art is usually not functional.

Q: In your work with illusion why is it important for you to use only analogue means? Even architecture is used in your works like a medium (an analogue one) through which you produce images.

S.W.:   What you can see on a screen I regard as a mediated reality. What is physically built is, for me, closer to reality. Architecture is a medium that we can experience in a haptical way. I am interested in sculptural qualities in the object. An installation can be seen as an image or as an object, so we can ask ourselves if it is an object that we perceive from the outside, or an installation that we perceive from the inside.

Q: Your works stage a conflictual state between what we expect to see, and the illusion behind it. Regarding also the fact that your works are always site-specific, where lies the polemic?

S.W.:   A good example in this sense is the work with the gallery desk in 'Gallery Coma' (Empfang, 2008), where I placed an imaginary mirror at the end of their reception desk, which was a literal doubling or mirroring of space. Here I have raised the question of the border between exhibition space and the area in which its commercialization takes place.

Fig. 4.30: Sinta Werner, Empfang, 2008, Installation view: 'The 3rd Floor', COMA, Berlin, ©Sinta Werner.

Fig. 4.31: Yukihiro Taguchi, Cave, 2010,
Galeria aM.4, Tokyo, ©Yukihiro Taguchi.

Interview with Yukiro Taguchi, October 2012

Q: What is the role of matter and materiality in the construction of these multiple realities
that you reveal in a single situation?

Y.T.:   'FABRIC/K', a work done in 2010 at the Program Gallery Berlin, together with
Vladimir Karaleev, has been a new experience for both of us. We did not initially know
which way each of us works, what techniques we each use and how we can join them,
so we made some rules: working only with fabric (this was interesting for me since I
wanted to experiment in this material), and spending working time in the gallery space
– each of us alone or together, changing the installation constantly. Karaleev worked in
a product design direction, while I worked on the material in my usual way. What I
was interested in was fabric, both as a surface, and in its quality of unifying things.
Absolutely everything has a surface that both unifies and separates things, but surface
is also a space in itself and, thinking about fabric, you can understand that it has its

own spatiality. Fabric can create volumes, and this is what we have worked on in this exhibition, but we have worked also on the texture. Fabric is flexible, and we showed its fluidity, as for example, in the installation in which a jacket encompassed the whole space. I am fascinated by fabrics because of their capacity to change. They can easily adapt to any idea, according to which, a piece of fabric can become everything: it can be a house – a tent, a cover, a container of any type. The fact that fabric is actually one single thread, a line, but also a surface, and it can be an entire space, all at the same time.

Q: So you are interested in the pluri-morphology of fabric? The fact that it can be at the same time volume, surface, the line of a thread, that it can fill an entire space and it can be at the same time invisible in separating spaces?

Y.T.:   Yes, and I am mostly preoccupied with its capacity to unite very different things, materialities etc.

I have also continued this work with fabrics in a non-commercial gallery space in Harajuku Tokyo, where I received fabrics sponsorship from the Tokyo Fashion Week. I have partially transformed them into clothes, but I always worked with them in a performative way, in the gallery space, on the streets, in parks, constantly building new installations. Then I showed the video with the performances at the opening of my show, as I had also done at the exhibition in Program. In Tokyo, I also let others perform their shows in the framework of my installation, which always kept changing its appearance.

I continued the work with fabric in small actions as well. At the breakfast at a friend's, for example, I sewed a jacket that continued into the table cloth on which the food was spread, and I myself performed in a casual rhythm, while joining in the breakfast.

Q: Could you explain the relationship between human agency and the force of matter in your work? Humans seldom appear in your work, whereas materials and objects have a voluntary force and their own force of motion that makes them move like humans.

Y.T.:   Actually my works are more about an exterior force that moves the objects, since they actually do not move alone. In my videos I do not show the entire process of movement, I cut out certain parts, so my agency seems to be an interior force that moves the objects. What I am interested in is to show the life that is in these objects. Every object has a unique character, a certain expression, due to its particular history, and this is also what I am searching for in objects. It is exactly this personal, cultural or social history of things that formulates the difference between each of them. What I

Fig. 4.32: Yukihiro Taguchi, Moment, 2009, 5th Vento Sul Biennial, Curitiba, Brasil, ©Yukihiro Taguchi.

Fig. 4.33 – 4.35: Yukihiro Taguchi,
Contact, 2009, Rio de Janeiro, Brasil,
©Yukihiro Taguchi.

want to show is the dynamic of an object from when it was produced until now, when and where we perceive it as *present*. I wish to show its route in time. This permanent movement in which objects are caught is actually invisible. It is the same with me (as the backstage force moving the objects and situations), since I am also caught in these movements, but this also stays unnoticed, invisible.

Q: Your architectural experiments show how a single construction can be transformed into many different constructions and abodes with the same amount of material that not only saves material, but also extends the functions of the initial house. These new constructions have many uses, are placed around the entire city and are ecological in the sense that they respond to the specificity of the environment.

Y.T.: Yes my work is mainly about these strategies, but also about their relation to the people, which I have also involved in different ways in this work. Each one of them develops his own activities in these temporary spaces. In my work for the '5th VentoSul Biennial' in Curitiba, Brazil, in 2009, I made the 'Moment Nr. 3' installation, and as I was not actually given an exhibition space, I worked in an almost ruined house in the open air. I then showed the work while building my own shelter out of the material of the house that had been dismantled, and I have placed it in the inner yard of the museum where the Biennial took place. Inside my shelter construction I showed video works with the destruction/construction process of the house.

Q: Viewing the transformations of the initial house, throughout your video we can also take a tour of the city of Curitiba. It is this fixity of a house, as a defining condition of a building, that you transform into a mobile device of circulation. How long have you been working on this video, and how long on this process of traversing the city of Curitiba with your installation?

Y.T.: It took me actually around two months! In Rio de Janeiro I created another work, which involved both performance and a video piece, and which is also based on human presence, but in a slightly different way. It is called 'Contact' and it shows me passing a message between two people, which stand half 100 meters away from each other. The message is in Brazilian, which I do not speak and I run as fast as I can from one to the other, in order not to forget the message on the way. I am, in this case, a sort of human mobile phone, replacing technical achievement with my personal effort. I have shown the piece with a three-channel projection: the perspectives of the two characters, and the other one showing me running, and the entire scene set beside the sea. I have not used the stop-motion technique here, but three fixed cameras and real time. The performance and the video lasted 30 minutes.

Q: It seems as if you are a messenger from late Antiquity that transmits letters or runs to the point of exhaustion to pass on a message.[15]

Y.T.: Actually the theme of the group exhibition where I showed this work was 'Communication' and it was sponsored by the telephone company in Rio de Janeiro. I wanted to see how we could transform this digitalized communication into a total analogue mode of transmission of information.

Q: Reproducing digital techniques with analogue also recalls your work 'Cave', shown in the Gallery αM in Tokyo in 2010, where you made projections with shadows that became the medium of representation. This immaterial construction alludes to Plato's cave, but in your work there is no primary light, the sun, instead the whole shadow game is based on created, borrowed, reflected light (mirrored light or recorded light).

Y.T.: In this installation the construction process consists of layering shadows, building a spatial construction with light and projections installed in superpositions: I have also placed shadows in shadows of different intensities that assemble the construction. I have noticed that in this work that builds a spatial environment out of shadows, the audience does not always actually observe the installation. People are generally very oriented towards objects, they look for objects and question less the space in itself. They search for meaning in the assemblage of elements, but do not question the space in its totality as an installation. This experience was interesting for me. I changed the installation every day. Thinking about the connection between the allegory of the cave and the specificity of pre-historic drawing, I have been transforming a Lascaux drawing of a horse, into a three-dimensional figure, projected as a shadow on the wall. I have also worked with time when projecting a flower, tracing its silhouette on the wall in pencil on the first day of the exhibition, and then drawing over the contours of its shadow over time, when the flower languished and changed its position. The marks showed the duration of the exhibition, but also alluded to death and the layering of time and extinction.

I also wanted to show that what we believe as being authentic can be actually another projected reality, which we assume as real, out of a pre-formed reaction. I created a cave-effect, in the sense of an environment where I do not point to any piece as a piece

Fig. 4.36: Yukihiro Taguchi, Cave, 2010, Galeria aM.4, Tokyo, ©Yukihiro Taguchi.

of art standing for an idea, but I point up *representation* itself. This is why I was also interested in the fact that at the beginning the audience was hardly able to look at the work in its totality, but was searching for meaning in its individual pieces, so I have tried to direct their attention to the process of representation through shadows.

Q: How did you understand Plato's allegory in relation to your work, and the stages of understanding that he describes as 'imagination', 'belief' and the final realization of the 'forms of the good'?

Y.T.: What is important for me is the idea that we interpret as real something which is in fact a projection, out of partial knowledge of a certain situation, which for me is not at all negative, but on the contrary is a fact that is carrying a lot of potential. All these steps that the prisoners in Plato's allegory traverse: being in front of a projection and not being able to turn their heads; seeing the marionette players after that and understanding that it had been a projection; and then finally seeing the sun as the ultimate cause of everything around, are for me proofs of the multiplicity of experience and the multiplicity of meaning and not signs of our incapacity of understanding. What I am able to extract as meaning from a situation is not everything that the situation carries: the situation ultra-passes the present and its interpretation, which is for me a very comforting thought, in itself a positive thought, but of course with negative aspects due to our incapacity to grasp entirely the reality. I am interested in the effects of this plurality of meaning and experience over each of us as individuals, with our system of thought, and I am also interested in how we can provoke this multiplicity in our thinking regarding the world.

Q: Your work in Kenya is different from your approaches before. What caused you to change your way of working, and how did your method adapt to the reality encountered there?

Y.T.: In Kenya, I was invited by a group of Japanese people who have an ecological farm that they run in collaboration with local people. I was not so much interested in creating a work of art, but in connecting with what I encountered there, in the sense of filming the work done by people, their rhythm of life: 'Made in Kenya, Sound of pond' (2012). I would like to work in a practical way with the people living there and make a video series with quotidian moments called 'Made in Kenya'.

Q: Your work is very conceptual, but you attain this through a very intensive, accurate and assiduous *manual* manner of working. This is at the same time connected to an

Fig. 4.37: Yukihiro Taguchi, Made in Kenya, Sound of pond, 2012, Performance, Kenya, ©Yukihiro Taguchi.

analogue approach to resolve the situations you are working on. Still you always amplify the given situation with a conceptual dimension that practically *surpasses* its physical possibilities.

Y.T.:   I am working manually and analogue firstly because I like the material dimension of the environment around me, and secondly because I like to have an un-mediated contact with it. Also if I carry out an action myself, with my own physical strength or endurance, it is this individual gesture that counts and I am interested in the uniqueness of any act. It is also another type of memory of your environment that you develop, if you engage physically with it. Also I perceive this work as a sort of training, through repetition and continuity. I also tend to reduce to a minimum all the intermediary material that I would need if I were to replace my work with various devices. I am discovering ways of doing everything by myself, which also changes the nature of the objects: for example I make the paper that I need myself. We always forget the way that the products that we buy daily are made, and why they have a certain appearance, and we forget what brought them into our hands: the meat that we buy, for example. If you deal with that meat manually through all the steps in the process of it arriving at the selling points, the fact that you interacted with it in a physical way will not let you forget the process. There are certain points at which I wish to interfere with the world in this manual way, in order to understand it in another way than usual.

Q: The paradox in your work – the fact that it seems that the objects move alone, but in fact it is only you, with your physical force, that make them move – is in this case actually a false paradox. What actually moves the objects is a *recording* of different processes that they have been through. You work with *a storage of time*, with the memory of these movements. And this particular sense of recording time is also analogue. But you are also slowing time down.

Y.T.:   Exactly! This is my movement. It is a time for thinking. I am not against involving digital means in my work, I actually make use of digital techniques, for which I am very grateful, but I am pleading for a reflexive use of them. I am searching in my work for ways of thinking about them, and having a more modest attitude about what is around.

Q: This reflexive use of means is also another method of slowing time down.

Y.T.:   In the industrial revolution, for example, through the involvement of technology on a daily basis, social life was definitely speeded up. The serialization of objects brought another perception of the object in time as well. We can think that time has always been perceived in different ways, according to cultural representation, but also according to material culture.

Interview with Michael Krome, July 2009

Q: Simulacrum is a concept that Bunga uses in order to define his work, mentioning that his work belongs to the domain of the simulacrum. How do you interpret the idea of simulacrum in relation to Bunga's work?

In connection with this, how do you understand the way Bunga works with the real? His constructions are simulacra of reality?

M.K.: Thinking about the concept of simulacrum, I find it open for temporalization. For me, a simulacrum is active on a temporal axis, as opposed to virtuality that designates an image, a representation from a medial point of view. The concept of simulacrum carries implications of a prospective and retrospective nature. In the case of Carlos's work, I am not sure if it functions only in a prospective way, in the sense that his constructions are models of something that will come.

Q: His drawings, for example, can be considered retrospective, in the sense that something *could have been* […].

M.K.: Yes, something that could have been or even that *has been*: the melancholia. His way of temporalizing melancholia is connected to what could have been or to what already was.

I connect his work also to construction measures that generate what can be seen as prospective ruins, unfinished constructions with many building problems that are not approved and remain deserted in the landscape: half-built torsos, which are broken and fall down. In Belgium or Italy we often see entire settlements that, due to financial crises or poor planning, stand on their concrete foundations like ghosts, and there are no funds left to completely break them down. I have always found these prospective ruins of the future more interesting than ruins of the past that erode, decay and fall down as part of a natural process. Regarding the work of Carlos, I think that the idea of simulacrum can be understood in both ways: forwards and backwards on the time scale. His drawings on reproductions of already realized works are retrospective interventions, but they are also connected to the future.

Q: You said that you understand virtuality as connected to space and the simulacrum as connected to time? Virtuality seems to me closer to our lived reality from a temporal point of view, just that it belongs to another spatiality, whereas a simulacrum is visually similar to the reality but belongs to other temporal sequences (the past, the present).

M.K.: Yes, that's right. Simulacrum seems to me more open to various scenarios in time with different narrative aspects than virtuality, which is occupied with the theory of media, by the idea of fake, by bipolar and dualistic principles.

Q: How do you interpret Carlos's use of material in connection with this problematic? Cardboard is a perishable material, but it is also a material that has a history of reproducing and faking more stable materials.

M.K.: I've talked to Carlos about his use of material and understand that he does not centre his art on the use of cardboard, which would reduce the potential of his work. I am personally interested in the socio-historical definition of materials, and questions about this new, trivial material are worth following up. When did it become popular, and how did the industrial realization of cardboard become a customary product? The history of cardboard is connected to the history of logistics, of transport and the packaging industry. It is connected to movement, to speed, but also to cheap mass production. But I think that Carlos is not interested in these aspects of the use of the cardboard as a material, in connotations of *arte povera* and *bricolage*. I believe that he is also not interested in a very tactile and haptic approach.

Q: Do you consider his constructions to be the expression of an architectural vision, in the sense of an architectural proposal with a certain finality? Or rather as environments that react to the situation in which they are placed and whose outcome remains open? And in relation to this, how do you understand the position that Bunga assumes towards his work, his auctorial statement?

M.K.: Is it not always a question of format, where the author is substituted for by the work? It is a process of delegation, where the author is delegated to the space, to the exhibition and the object of display, and in this way the control of the author over the work and over its reception disappears. I have the impression that Bunga's understanding of art, his *ductus*, the melancholy that appears in all his works is inherent to the disappearance, the inexistence, the death of the author.

Bunga is also an artist who does not wish to exercise too much control over the work, or over the reaction of the audience. With control as an artist, you have more certainty that the work is not misunderstood. In any artistic process misunderstandings, and loss of images and circumstances where the work does not function, can occur. Also there are always moments when we lose comprehension and the work itself disappears. In this sense I appreciate an author's modesty in the transmission of his art, believing that one cannot understand everything and that art has its own *physis*. I consider this in Bunga's work as a form of liberality. Also, of great interest for me is understanding how the concept of the political enters his work. I think that in his work art does not intend to cause or determine something in the didactic way that usually happens. He is very interested in the political implications, but he can keep the process open, he does not intend to control it, while the process of creation stays very organic.

Interview with Hironari Kubota, November 2011

Q: 'Senju-Kannon' (2012), the work you created in 'Centro Cultural de Belem', in Lisbon, is a confluence of elements from various traditions and time frames. Please talk about them and explain why you brought them together?

H.K.: 'Senju-Kannon' is an object of worship in Buddhism. Until now, my work was about spinning cars and ships, although I had the idea to spin an idol three years ago. And now I had the opportunity, so I created the piece. My artworks have always had elements of Shinto or nature worship, where there is no worship of gods or idols. I give various connotations to the concept of idol. When I went to Lithuania, I saw the statue of Lenin, just as I saw Tito's statue in Yugoslavia. They impressed me a lot, because they have similarities with the iconography of religious idols, and the way they are presented is similar to that of an object of worship. That is why I think it would be also interesting to work with these symbols in the countries to

Fig. 4.38: Hironari Kubota, The Man Maid
Lake, 2011, ©Hironari Kubota.

Fig. 4.39: Hironari Kubota, The spinning car in Ricefields, 2012, ©Hironari Kubota.

whose cultures they belong. This time I chose to work with a Japanese idol here in Portugal, but I would be interested to work also with a local religious symbol, to explore more the domain of Catholicism. When I spun a Trabant car in Berlin, parts of the audience of my show thought the subject was cruel and too intense, since it is a symbol of the former East Germany's communist past, but it is also so intimately connected to the life of the people in recent times. I'm asking myself whether it's moral to cause such a strong reaction. Since I am not aware of the deep reality here in Portugal, I wasn't confident about working on a piece with a religious symbolic connotation, with whom people could strongly identify.

Q: How would the spinning of the idol be received in Japan?

H.K.: In Japan, I don't think that I would upset many people by spinning 'Senju-Kannon' because the audience would make a differentiation, which I am not sure would be perceived in a European context. The difference comes from the fact that I don't spin an original Kannon from a temple, which would indeed upset some people, but a Kannon *reproduced* by me, which would not be perceived as offensive. Another general cultural difference that influences the reception of the work is the connotation of the materials used: I realized that people in Portugal didn't associate Styrofoam with penurious means. In Japan I would be more interested to sculpt a Kannon in a tree stem and spin it, and not do it in Styrofoam, as I did in Lisbon. In Japan, Styrofoam is often used in TV production, and is therefore perceived as cheap and connected to consumption, which is a connotation that I do not wish to transmit and would impede me from putting across the message I intend for the audience in Japan.

Q: Do you usually work with cultural symbolism? Or is it more a personal understanding of these symbols that you transmit in your work?

H.K.: I always used symbols in my artworks, for example in my work with Dankon, which is the prehistoric phallic worship of ancestors in Japan. They worship 'Dankon' as the symbol of fertility, reproduction and fortune. Of great importance for me is a festival that takes place where I grew up in Suwa, Nagano: 'Onbashira matsuri'. At this festival, large trees are cut off and pulled for 20 to 30 kilometres, with human power, without technology, to a Shinto shrine. Each tree weighs ten metric tonnes, and pulling them is practically impossible, but it is still performed ritually every year. Still, the festival is meant to show that humans are powerless in the face of nature, and people experience the awe of nature and feel the existence of God and respect for nature. Of course the connotation of God differs across the country, between Shintoism, Buddhism and their various branches. The experience of animism, as it is transmitted in this festival, where trees are perceived as holy, is rooted in my works. Where I grew up, cars were dumped and abandoned in nature. Cars were covered in tree leaves and ivies, rusting away. I saw the cars as a part of nature as a child, and only now do I perceive it as a chipped junk of iron, and this is what made me pick up abandoned cars and spin them. When I spin objects with high velocity, I notice people experiencing danger, but also a state of inner confusion, while seeing beyond the common vehicle: the car, changing into something else. This experience of transformation is similar to the contemplation of an idol, or another symbolically charged figure. What I find most interesting is the fact that no matter what object is spun, the effect of its fast spinning is transcending the object and its image into something else, which becomes unrecognizable. I want to provoke that moment of experience in which people, carried away by confusion, see something else in this object.

Q: I noticed also that the rhythm with which you were spinning the Kannon in the Lisbon work changed slightly, and a disassociation of sound and image took place. It was like time slipping from the 'now' into sometime else. Was it an intentional device you used?

H.K.: When I spun the Kannon, I changed the run speed of the motor and the background music. People told me they were taken away from the present, as in time travel. I use old Japanese popular music 'Enka' as background music and combine two songs that last for around five minutes. While spinning the idol I change the speed and pitch of the music and this causes people to perceive the work and its environment differently. In that sense, my work might entail the act of turning time or 'changing' time, as if time slipped. Some might recall their childhood and home town, some might imagine ancient times.

Q.:   On the other hand, your work is also connected to a strong material expressivity of the elements you are working with.

H.K.:   The forces that emanate from each material are completely different. Whether it's iron, tree, stone, Styrofoam or the air, the force and spirit of each is completely different, and when working with them I feel that I have to deal with their different responsiveness. What I intend to do is to work with these elements in an unexpected way – to me that's what is important. I am also working with the beliefs that people have, for example, about cars. These beliefs are themselves a force. It is not only the force of the material itself, but the thoughts of people on certain topics that represent a strong power. That's what I am interested in working with. Cars are not just metal. People have certain images and conceptions about the objects and these have a strength that is very difficult to break. In my work I engage with the power of these unexpressed pre-formed thoughts; I react to them and I try to modulate them in my performances.

On the other hand, what I also intend is to stay true to the essence and expressivity of materials such as trees and iron. But at the same time, I need to be sensitive about people's conception and beliefs about certain symbols. I do not wish to offend. Depending on the way in which I work with them, I first need to understand what people see in the symbol.

Q: Can you talk about other works of yours from this perspective?

H.K.:   For example, in 'Heroes of Tragedy' (1997), a piece that I made 15 years ago, I welded iron plates together, and constructed them into a sculpture that moves slowly. When welding the iron, I wanted to use a method used for pottery in the Jomon period[16] – the joining of small tiles into a big piece. During my long working process, I welded iron tiles into an object of about three metres tall that I wanted to bring into motion, so I incorporated a machine for road construction into it that makes the piece move slowly. While welding and interacting with iron, I learned about it and how I could make it move forward. And I think it was also something about me wanting to move forward. It did not have the implications of an object of worship, but it was more about interacting with ancient times and enlivening the ancient method of pottery-making.

When I moved to Tokyo (and I still don't like big cities like Tokyo), I felt the danger of standardization. I became interested in my history and background and I started creating pieces connected to the local culture in my home town. I started realizing that the inspiration for my works actually comes from Onbashira Matsuri.[17] While researching, I became aware of the impact of the Jomon period on my home town Suwa, Nagano, and the prosperity that it brought in that period. I found out about their use of masks in these festivals, and I started working on masks in order to understand them better. I wanted to make a big moving object and I picked up and collected trees that are suited to carving and sculpting that had usually been blown down by typhoons. In 'Illusory Race' (1999), I made masks from these trees while trying to keep the expression of the material alive. I realized then that materials speak to me and that it was very important for me to let this interaction be effective and operate in my pieces.

'The Mighty Paradise' (1999) was the first piece in which I spun a car, along with very loud music, and audiences looked at this dangerous and uncontrollable object with excitement. Then I realized its expression and effect on people resembled moments from Onbashira Matsuri. Loud background music is also connected to my experiences with the festival in my home town. We also have a dance festival called Bon Odori that is important in my work. In August, during the period called Bon, people believe their ancestors' spirits come back to where we are. To celebrate, people gather and dance to really loud music in a shrine or in a temple.

When I went back to my home town as an adult, I actually realized the huge contrast between the tranquillity of the village and this really loud music at night. At Onbashira Matsuri, 1000 people try to pull heavy trees, and in order to cheer them on, and to prompt people to reunite and work together, they usually perform what is called Kiyari, a type of shouting and cheering. Trumpets are also blown to stimulate teamwork. This kind of music was also used in wars, as well, to encourage soldiers to attack. During my performances at first I used to play children's pop music such as Doraemon, but then people don't attribute much importance to the lyrics, and they just think of it as a funny experience. So I started using old Japanese popular music, Enka, thinking that the audience would be able to identify more with the lyrics.

I was always interested in Japanese history and historic periods such as the Sengoku period and the Meiji Ishin, and I draw my thoughts from the changes that they brought.[18]

Q: In your works you involve often your own bodily force. Is engaging your body in your performances a means of personal self-expression, or rather do you conduct or channel the action that is taking place?

H.K.: In 'The Smell of Mud II' (2004), for example, I got a tattoo on my back of the picture of the famous samurai Yoshida Shounin,[19] which was a long and painful process and took six months to complete. Yoshida Shounin had lived in the period just before Meiji Ishin. He was the first person to realize the need to change the Japanese political system, and he was keen on the influence of foreign countries, which finally brought him to his execution. He was an educator who inspired youngsters to provoke a revolution. He also developed a philosophical direction of thought, which was very influential at that time, and which was called *yomei gaku*, a neo-Confucianism based on the teachings of Wang Yangming. His belief was that when there is an instinctive need to act, it has to be constantly practised. Being sincere to his idea, he inspired people and became the catalyst energy of the upcoming revolution in Japan. Nowadays he is considered a symbol of right wing power, but I am totally against this nationalist interpretation and I would like to demonstrate the confusion behind it. When he turned 30, he was executed. In my 20s, when I had this tattoo done, I was strongly inspired by his philosophy that informed my art, and I perceived that

I was drawing vital energy from him to continue working. When I turned 30 a time of change in my life and art happened, I started to travel and perform a lot overseas, so I decided to remove the tattoo. Still I thought that a respectful way to remove the tattoo of Yoshida Shounin was not to laser-erase it easily, but to remove it through a long process: a performance that I executed in a tattoo booth in Paris. I thought it was important for me to feel this process physically with the natural pain that is attached to it, so I decided not to remove the tattoo, but to cover it up and paint it black. What resulted is a big black square on my back that has stayed there ever since.

Video Interview. Camera: Fernando Veiras
Many thanks to Feranando Veiras, Yuko Yamamoto and Fukuda Yuichi for conducting this interview, and their precious assistance in the realization of Senju-Kannon.
Translation from recording in Japanese by Masae Yamazaki.

NOTES

1   This video can be accessed online: Yukihiro Taguchi (2008), Last Chair, https://www.youtube.com/watch?v=oAtfegtI2vM&index=3&list=PL1DACC0446390D027 (last accessed April 2014).

2   For Heim virtuality as art is a metaphysical, esoteric dimension, which cannot be reduced to technological progress and optimization. He compares the virtual world with the Gesamtkunstwerk/The Total Artwork of Richard Wagner. The Gesamtkunstwerk is not only a form of poetry or entertainment, or a joining of various domains of art, but is also a new form of reality, which transforms the existent understanding of reality fundamentally. The parallel with Wagner's Gesamtkunstwerk is part of his effort to identify the specific thinking that led to the appearance of digital reality in past cultural manifestations.

3   For a further bibliography, and other theoreticians of the virtual and cyberspace, see also Bell et al. (2004).

4   'Out of Hand. Materializing the Postdigital' at MAD New York, on view between October 16, 2013 to June 1, 2014

5   For Deleuze prehension is when: 'an element is the given, the 'datum' of another element that prehends it; the registering of another entity through the qualities of the prehending object. Prehension is individual unity. Everything prehends its antecedents and concomitants and, by degrees, prehends a world. The eye is a prehension of light. Living beings prehend water, soil, carbon and salts. At a given moment the pyramid prehends Napoleon's soldiers (forty centuries are contemplating us), and inversely'. (Deleuze 2006b: 88).

6   For Leibniz the world is made up of monads, which can be understood also as points of perception. Leibniz regards every being as its own perception of the world, while each perceiving monad is an expression of one being. Deleuze reinforces Leibniz's concept of the monad, stating that the world is a pure emission of

singularities. For both Leibniz and Deleuze monads are simple substances, indivisible and indestructible, while the world is constituted by them (see various entries in Parr 2005).

7   For further references, see Vogl (2007).

8   For a further bibliographical reference on the actualization of the virtual in Deleuze, see Ott (2007).

9   Boris Groys (2008) also writes about the production of the new, connected to the archiving of cultural material and to the production of contemporary art. He associates the poly-semantic condition of contemporary work (medially and conceptually paradoxical) to the production of the new and assigns its authority to the balance of power that it mirrors. The pluralism of the contemporary art is not permissive and inclusive, but is based, in Groys view, on a permanent inclusion–exclusion. The starting point of the inner paradox of contemporary art is, for Groys, the modern object of Duchamp, which is at the same time art and non-art. Groys argues that modern art has attempted to find a balance of power in artwork, whereas paradoxical contemporary art is surpassing any limitations of taste and power, showing the intention to step outside the art system, while actually staying rooted in it (Groys 2008: 3).

It is precisely in this paradox that Groys sees the origin of the new:

'The modern artwork positioned itself as a paradox-object also in this deeper sense – as an image and as a critique of the image at the same time […] The desire to get rid of any image can be realized only through a new image — the image of a critique of the image'. (Groys 2008: 9)

For Groys the new is the alive/the vivid in art, which is considered to be outside the museum, the archive or the library. Groys argues in his essay 'On the New' (Groys 2008: 23–43) that the act of collecting in museums determines that art always has to seek the new, the alive, the real, in order to museify it. (Groys 2008: 25)

As something totally new cannot be assimilated, and since the new cannot be recognized through the totally different, then for Groys the only way to manifest the new is to use the same, the identical or the equal that will make it recognizable as new (Groys 2008: 30). According to Groys this is the ready-made, which blurs the difference between new and old. For Groys, the new is therefore a reminder that the difference between the original and the simulation always stays ambiguous, that the doubt on the nature of things cannot be surpassed. (Groys 2008: 41)

10   In his book Camille (1996) explains that due to this confusing unreality of the simulacrum, in the Middle Ages it was used to designate something untrue, and therefore also it referred to the idols of 'the others' (the saint or other holy figures of the Jews or Muslims).

11   Contrary to the vision of Deleuze, who recognizes the simulacrum as a positive opening towards other critical interpretations, Jean Baudrillard dedicates his writings to the concept of the simulacrum in an apocalyptic tone. He applies the concept to the social context and relates it to his fatalistic vision of the present. 'Simulacra and simulations' (Baudrillard 1988: 166–184) starts with a passage that has been extensively cited in the context of contemporary art, the essay 'The precession of simulacra'. Simulation is, for Baudrillard, more than an illusion, which is faking the 'false' by letting it seem real, while keeping the original reality intact. Simulation, on the contrary, means for him the destruction of an original reality, which shakes up the distinction between true and false. In Baudrillard's consideration, this destruction of the truth through simulation, after the effects of the all-encompassing simulation, causes the world to be emptied of meaning. The simulacrum – as a product

of this process by which reality has been undermined – is a coherent world in itself, but a world in which empty signs point to themselves, and meaning and value are absent. From the perspective of its viewer, this world is a means of abduction in the dimension of the visual, behind which there is nothing else to find. The media has a definitive role in this game: it simulates the simulacrum reality, which is not a mediation, but the reinforcement of a closed circle. Another source on Baudrillard's thinking on the simulacrum is: Baudrillard, J. (2007), *Das Ereignis,* Schriften aus dem Kolleg Friedrich Nietzsche, Weimar: Verlag der Bauhaus Universität Weimar. The two chapters *Event 1* and *Event 2* discuss the relationship of the virtual with the event. In the context of this volume, it is relevant that Baudrillard discusses the problem of documentation as an anticipatory means to influence the nature of the event itself, even if it is perceived after that as retrospective (for his argumentation he is having as a starting point some films broadcast before the 9/11 event in the United States). The image adopts, therefore, the function of simulation and documentation at the same time.

12   The term *différance* goes back to a lecture that Derrida held in January 1968 at the *Société française de philosophie* (see: Derrida 1988b). The meaning of the term *différance* is found in the difference between the two nouns *différance* and *différence.* Contrary to *différence,* the newly invented concept designates Derrida's insight that the differences originate in a game of relationships and that, instead of an original (in relation to which a difference is normally formulated), only the traces of this original are left. The space of these relationships that emerges is always open and borders are dissolved. The insight that the meaning is not fixed for any utterance comes with the understanding of *différance,* but it is deferred with every new fixing of the relationship. The identity and the meaning of an utterance are always transformable.

13   Hironari Kubota's is referring his performances during which his heavy sculptures and installations start to move, spin or move forward in space, through the force of the artist or an exterior motor.

14   Parts of this interview with Carlos Bunga appeared as Jecu (2010).

15   See here for example Philip Rousseau (2012). These messengers were actually responsible for the right delivery of the content and they represented the absent author's voice. They were actually not only transmitters, but also often participators at the exchange, being asked to give replies in the name of their master.

16   The Jomon period is a prehistoric time in Japan known for its pottery culture.

17   Onbashira (御柱祭) is a festival held every six years in the Lake Suwa area of Nagano, Japan. The purpose of the festival is to symbolically renew the Suwa Taisha or Suwa Grand Shrine. 'Onbashira' can be literally translated as 'the honored pillars'. The Onbashira festival is reputed to have continued, uninterrupted, for 1200 years. The festival is held once every six years, in the years of the Monkey and the Tiger in the Chinese Zodiac; however, the locals may say 'once every seven years', because of the traditional Japanese custom of including the current year when counting a period of time. Onbashira lasts several months, and consists of two moments: Yamadashi and Satobiki. Yamadashi traditionally takes place in April, and Satobiki takes place in May. 'Yamadashi' literally means 'coming out of the mountains'. During this part of the festival, huge trees are cut down in a Shinto ceremony using axes specially manufactured for this purpose. The stems are decorated in red-and-white regalia, the traditional colors of Shinto ceremonies, and ropes are attached to them. During Yamadashi, teams of men drag the logs down the mountain towards the four shrines of Suwa Taisha. The course of the logs goes

over rough terrain, and at certain points the logs must skid or be dropped down steep slopes. Young men prove their bravery by riding the logs down the hill in a ceremony known as 'Ki-otoshi' (see the webpage of the Festival: Onbashira (date unknown)).

18   The Sengoku period (middle of the 16th century–beginning of the 17th century) was a time of social upheaval, political intrigue, and constant military conflict that led to the unification of political power during the Tokugawa shogunate. Meiji Ishin (1868–1912) was a time of reform, when, under the emperor Meiji, Japan became a modernized nation, putting an end to the shogunate.

19   Yoshida Shoin was born in 1830 and died in 1859 in Tokyo. He was a distinguished intellectual and teacher in the last years of the Tokugawa shogunate.

Fig. 5.1: Carlos Bunga,
DESTERRITORIALIZACION, 2013,
Galeria Casas Riegner, Colombia,
©Carlos Bunga.

Conclusion

Jumping from one box into another to make his way through Galeria Casas Riegner in Bogota, 'deprived of territory', the visitor in Carlos Bunga's show 'Desterritorializacion' (2013) is insulated by the parameters of a booth. The space is organized in square cardboard boxes that, like a 19th-century urban plan, swallow the visitor in a both protecting and disorienting way. The visitor will have to perceive the world through the square format – like the main character of Kobo Abe's novel 'The Box Man', written in 1973 and set in Tokyo. The book is the diary of a man who decided to live on the streets in a box that covers him from head to the hips, from which he sees the world through an 'observation slit' of 35 mm. The original edition also provides an image: a 35-mm film fragment with the 'view' of the Box Man framed by cardboard on the upper and lower side. When he sits down, the box becomes a house. The novel begins with precise instructions on how to make a box: you need an empty box of corrugated cardboard, transparent vinyl to cover the 35-mm orifice, water-resistant rubber tape, a bit of wire and a pointed knife. As the Box Man explains, no striking feature should be allowed on the box, to preserve its 'special anonymity'. Wandering the streets of Tokyo, the box on his head gradually destabilizes his identity until he completely fuses with the inorganic nature of the box. The paper cabin, as Abe's book teaches, is a paradigmatic, universal form that is housing, hiding, moving and even producing a 35-mm film.

'Neither Man nor Box' (Abe 2001: 7) turns to be, without noticing even himself, the visitor of Carlos Bunga's installation in Bogota, which is made with no more than the materials and tools that Abe Kobo recommended.

This idea of a potent architecture (a box) that offers plural solutions has always been sought out: a house that is mobile, a man that is fused with his habitation, a container that has multiple functions, a hiding place that is at the same time a point of observation, an invisible abode that escapes social control. Beyond these *topoi* the works gathered in this volume are built to offer concrete solutions for situations that can be socially or organizationally optimized. In a minimal, lucid way, these works are also transmitting philosophical thoughts, the reason for which they are regarded here as theoretical sources. They show ways in which the accumulation of information layers (the history) existent in an environment, building or situation can be put into circulation again, augmenting its agency. Intervening in the existing social and urban structure with an altered architecture (like Abe Kobo's Box Man) is making use of the virtual potential that architecture carries. Different means by which this can be transformed into an active tool and can be experienced in a concrete, tactile way, in interdependency with its 'user', were followed throughout this book. Without aiming towards a direct reinforcement of theoreticians' texts with artists' statements (or vice versa), but at an affiliation of ideas, each chapter has extracted from the interviews and traced in related sources factors that have been considered fundamental by the artists in their way of conceiving an architecture expanded beyond its physical condition. Drawn together, these factors could also explain how the virtual can be experienced in a conceptual, yet materially convincing way.

Performativity, which establishes a connection between a subject and its environment, designates in this context the quality of architecture to 'act' – to be an active agent. From the broad literature connected to this subject, I resumed some theories that argue for the socially innovative potential of performativity. Constructing a work along this principle also determines a detachment of the author/artist from his work, which takes its own course of action while the context becomes part of it – also a consequence of the modern structure of the image. I connected this non-auctorial performative work in the second chapter with the 'architecture of the event' conceived by Jacques Derrida. An idea that this volume forwards is that the specific approach to architecture practised by these and similar artists represents a late materialization of the philosophical project of Jacques Derrida, for which the discipline itself did not find a functional solution in the 1980s. Connected to this deconstructive vision of architecture are also some of the concepts that they often invoke and that also mark the edge between the material and the virtual presence of architecture: the ruin (a fusion of construction and deconstruction processes in various historic epochs) and the monument – which, like an archive, is based on memory and its alteration (if personal, collective or political).

In the third chapter I sketch an access to the experience of the virtual in conceptualism and post-conceptualism. I identify a certain direction in conceptual art that set a high value on the material qualities of objects, partially by means of documentation, and which transgressed the limits of the so-called 'hard', totally abstract conceptualism. Connected to it are the voided environments with which these artists work and which are also linked to an old tradition of iconophobia and the destruction of artistic representation. On the other hand, documentation is engaged in these works as a means of deconstructing the object and bringing motion to matter, which is again performative. By invoking ideas expressed in the interviews and in the works, I show that post-conceptual documentation invented a mutated object that has contributed to the overlap between the virtual and the real.

The fourth chapter aims firstly at splitting the question of virtual–real from states of visibility and invisibility, connected to representation and mediality. The virtual is here connected to technology, derived from or independent from the digital, with the intention of identifying conditions of actualization of the virtual in which the virtual can directly 'change' the real. I draw notions mentioned in the previous chapters (like the event, a transformative object, a potentiality that exceeds the concrete object and performativity) into convergence in order to explain phenomena of emergence of the virtual. The influential writings of Gilles Deleuze explain a virtual which is independent of the digital. Mimesis and simulation (both means to express an unmanifested potential of an object and therefore to produce the virtual) are confronted in relation to the specific analogous *modus operandi* of the works.

This attempt to access the virtual from a post-digital 'posture' or to identify the possibility of actualization of the virtual in post-conceptual works (especially regarding architectural works and solutions in urban design) defends thinking in analogue terms about the virtual, while having assimilated the experience of the digital. Essentially my aim has been to address a recent phenomena, which replaces the speculations around a technological omnipotent digital object/architecture with a more conceptual approach. The materialization (even if only temporary) of a virtual potential is bound to a philosophical approximation to architecture and the object, which can be called post-digital. The works gathered here address not only the humanization of the digital thinking (by working with haptic experiences and basic building techniques). They also draw an interplay between embodied and augmented realities in an architecture that surpasses its material form, and is based on a coroboration of various intellectual trajectories .

But it is also the old 'DO IT' dictum of conceptual art that moves across these works: the metamorphoses of a box into a human or into architecture can induce a virulent effect.

> Just making the box is simple enough, at the outside it takes less than an hour. However it requires considerable courage to put the box on, over your head, and get to be a box man. Anyway, as soon as anyone gets into this simple, unpreposessing paper cubicle and goes out into the streets, he turns into an apparition that is neither man nor box. A box man possesses some offensive poison about him.

> (Abe 2001: 7)

REFERENCES

Abe, K. (2001), *The Box Man*, New York: Vintagebooks.

Andrew, Ian (2002), 'Post-digital Aesthetics', MAP-uts lecture, http://www.ian-andrews.org/texts/postdig.html. Accessed April 2014.

Austin, J. (1962), *How to do Things with Words*, London: Oxford University Press.

Bal, M. (ed.)(1999), *The Practice of Cultural Analysis*, Stanford: Stanford University Press.

——————(2009), 'Setting the stage; The subject mise-en-scene', in A. Serban, M. Duculescu (eds), *The Seductiveness of the Interval*, Stockholm: Romanian Cultural Institute, pp. 91–106.

Baudrillard, J. (1988), 'Simulacra and simulations', in M. Poster (ed.), *Jean Baudrillard, Selected Writings*, Stanford: Stanford University Press, pp. 166–184.

——————(2007), *Das Ereignis/The Event,* Weimar: Verlag der Bauhaus Universität Weimar.

Bell, D., Brain D., Pleace, N. and Schuler, D. (eds), (2004), *Cyberculture. The Key Concepts,* London: Routledge, p. 171.

Benjamin, W. (1936), *The Work of Art in the Age of Mechanical Reproduction*, chapter XIV, http://www.marxistp. org/reference/subject/philosophy/works/ge/benjamin.htm, UCLA School of Theater, Film and Television; Transcribed by Andy Blunden 1998; proofed and corrected February 2005. Accessed 28 May 2013.

——————(1989), 'Das Kunstwerk im Zeitalter seiner technischen Reproduzierbarkeit', in R. Tiedemann, H. Schweppenhäuser (eds), *Walter Benjamin Gesammelte Schriften*, Frankfurt: Suhrkamp, vol. VII, pp. 350–384.

Berggruen, O., Hollein, M., Pfeiffer, I. (2004), *Yves Klein, 1928–1962*, Frankfurt: Schirn Kunsthalle.

Bishop, C. (2001), *Installation Art,* London: Tate Publishing.

Böhme, G. (2004), 'Der Raum leiblicher Anwesenheit und der Raum als Medium der Darstellung', in S. Krämer (ed.), *Performativität und Medialität*, München: Wilhelm Fink, pp. 129–140.

Brunette, P., Wills, D. (eds) (1994), *Deconstruction and the Visual Arts: Art, Media, Architecture*, Cambridge: Cambridge University Press.

Busta, C. (2008), 'The actor's studio', http://www.mutualart.com/OpenArticle/The-Actor-s-Studio/0F85631C62862B93, *ArtForum International*, February Issue. Accessed 28 May 2013.

Butler, J. (1993), *Bodies that Matter: On the Discursive Limits of Sex,* London: Routledge.

——————(2001), 'Performative Akte und Geschlechterkonstitution', in U. Wirth (ed.), *Performanz*, Frankfurt am Main: Suhrkamp, pp. 301–323.

Camille, M. (1996), 'Simulacrum', in R. Nelson, R. Shiff (eds), *Critical Terms for Art History*, Chicago: University of Chicago Press.

Cascone, K. (2000), 'The Aesthetics of Failure: Post-Digital Tendencies in Contemporary Computer Music', in *Computer Music Journal*, 24:4, Winter 2000, Massachusetts Institute of Technology, pp. 12–18.

Centre George Pompidou (1983), *Yves Klein*, exhibition catalogue, Paris: Musee National d'art Moderne.

Copeland, M. (2009), (ed.), *Vides. Une Retrospective*, exhibition catalogue, Paris: Centre Pompidou.

Crary, J. (1996), *Techniken des Betrachters. Sehen und Moderne im 19 Jahrhundert*, Dresden: Verlag der Kunst.

——————(2002), *Aufmerksamkeit. Wahrnehmung und Moderne Kultur*, Frankfurt am Main: Suhrkamp.

Daskalova, R. (1997), 'Interview with Yoshio Shirakawa and Masachi Ogura', http://pagesperso-orange.fr/articide. com/gutai/fr/sy_om.htm. Accessed 21 May 2013.

------(date unknown), 'Interview with Yoshio Shirakawa and Masashi Ogura', http://pagesperso-orange.fr/articide.com/gutai/fr/sy_om.htm. Accessed 28 May 2013.

Deleuze, G. (1994), *Difference and Repetition*, New York: Columbia University Press.

------(2005), 'The simulacrum and ancient philosophy', in *Logic of Sense*, London: Continuum, pp. 291–303.

------(2006a), 'The actual and the virtual', in E.R. Albert (ed., trans.) *Deleuze Dialogues II*, London: Continuum, pp. 112–115.

------(2006b), *The Fold. Leibniz and the Baroque*, London: Continuum.

------(2007), *Henri Bergson, zur Einführung*, Dresden: Junius Verlag.

Derrida, J. (1988a), 'Signatur, ereignis, kontext', in P. Engelmann (ed.) *Randgänge der Philosophie*, Vienna: Passagen Verlag, pp. 291–314.

------(1988b), 'Die différance', in J. Derrida (ed.), *Randgänge der Philosophie*, Wien: Passagen, pp. 29–52.

------(1989b), 'Fifty-two aphorisms for a foreword', in A. Papadakis, C. Cooke, A. Benjamin (eds), *Deconstruction*, New York: Rizzoli International Publications, pp. 67–72.

------(1991), *Mémoires d'aveugle, L'autoportrait et autres ruines,* Paris: Réunion des Musées Nationaux.

------(1992), *Die Wahrheit in der Malerei*, Wien: Passagen Verlag.

------(1997a), 'Why Peter Eisenman writes such good books', in N. Leach (ed.), *Rethinking Architecture. A Reader on Cultural Theory*, London, New York: Routledge, pp. 336–347.

------(1997b), 'Point de Folie – Maintenant l' Architecture' – Section 3, in N. Leach (ed.), *Rethinking Architecture. A Reader on Cultural Theory*, London, New York: Routledge, pp. 324–336.

------(1998a), *Archive Fever,* Chicago: University of Chicago Press.

------(1998b), 'Seminar Speech at the University of the Witwatersrand, Johannesburg', *(direct transcription by Verne Harris),* in C. Hamilton, H. Verne, R. Graeme (2002), (eds), *Refiguring the Archive*, Cape Town: Clyson Printers.

Derrida, J. and Meyer, E. (1997), 'Architecture where the desire may leave – A dialogue', in N. Leach (ed.), *Rethinking Architecture. A Reader on Cultural Theory*, London, New York: Routledge, pp. 319–323.

Derrida, J. and Norris, C. in Discussion (1989a), in A. Papadakis, C. Cooke, A. Benjamin (eds), *Deconstruction*, New York: Rizzoli International Publications, pp. 71–75.

Dimendberg, E. (1994), 'The museum as liquid space', in Jacobson, Karen (eds), *Expressionist Utopias*, exhibition catalogue, California: Los Angeles County Museum of Art and University of California Press.

Druckrey, T. (ed.), (1996), *Electronic Culture, Technology and Visual Representation,* New York: Aperture.

Duschek, K. (ed.), (1997), *Zero und Paris 1960, und heute*, Stuttgart: Hatje Cantz.

Edensor, T. (2005), *Industrial Ruins, Space Aesthetics and Materiality*, Oxford: Berg Publishers.

Ehrlicher, H. (2001), *Die Kunst der Zerstörung. Gewaltfantasien und Manifestationspraktiken europäischer Avantgarden*, Berlin: Akademie Verlag.

Eisenman, P. (1989), 'An architectural design interview by Charles Jencks', in A. Papadakis, C. Cooke, A. Benjamin (eds), *Deconstruction*, New York: Rizzoli International Publications, pp. 141–149.

Eng, M. (2003), *Sancho Silva. Film Machine*, http://sancho-silva.blogspot.pt/2007/04/film-machine-michael-eng-2003.html. Accessed 28 May 2013.

Felman, Shoshana (1983), *The Literary Speech Act. Don Juan with J. L. Austin, or Seduction in Two Languages,* New York: Cornell University Press.

Flusser, Vilem (2004): "Digital Apparition", in Timothy Druckrey (ed.) (1996): *Electronic Culture*, pp. 242–245.

Foster, H. (1996), '*The Return of the Real. Critical Models in Art and Theory Since 1960*', Massachusetts: The MIT Press.

Gamboni, D. (2002), 'Image to destroy, indestructible image', *Iconoclash*, http://hosting.zkm.de/icon/stories/storyReader$15. Accessed 28 May 2013.

Godfrey, T. (2006), 'What happened next in conceptual art: Chapter eleven', *Contemporary Journal, 21*:85, www.contemporary-magazines.com/profile85_1.htm. Accessed 28 May 2013.

Greenberg, C. (1989), *Art and Culture: Critical Essays*, Boston: Beacon Press.

——————(2000), *Homemade Esthetics: Observations on Art and Taste*, Oxford, New York: Oxford University Press.

Grosz, E. (2001), 'The future of space: Toward an architecture of invention', in P. Weibel (ed.), *Olafur Eliasson: Surroundings Surrounded*, Cambridge, Massachusetts: The MIT Press, pp. 252–268.

Groys, B. (2000), *Unter Verdacht, Eine Phänomenologie der Medien*, München, Wien: Carl Hanser Verlag.

——————(2008), *Art Power,* Cambridge Massachusetts, London: The MIT Press.

Gutai (1956), 'Manifesto', Ashiya City Museum of Art & History , http://web.archive.org/web/20070630202927/http://www.ashiya-web.or.jp/museum/10us/103education/nyumon_us/manifest_up.htm. Accessed 21 May 2013.

Hantelmann, D. v. (2001), 'Inszenierung des Performativen in der zeitgenössischen Kunst', *Paragrana* 10:1, pp. 255–270.

——————(2007), *How to Do Things with Art*, Berlin: Diaphanes.

Heim, M. (1993), *The Metaphysics of Virtual Reality*, Oxford, New York: Oxford University Press.

Hirata, T. (2009), 'Yukihiro Taguchi, Über performative sketch', in *Kalonsnet Magazine*, 07/Dec, http://www.kalons.net/index.php?option=com_content&view=article&id=506&catid=&lang=us. Accessed 28 May 2013.

Hollander, D. (2002), 'Puncturing genres. Barthes and Derrida on the limits of representation', in W. Wurzer (ed.), *Panorama, Philosophies of the Visible*, London, New York: Continuum, pp. 34–40.

Iser, W. (1998), 'Mimesis – Emergenz', in A. Kablitz, G. Neumann (eds), *Mimesis und Simulation*, Freiburg im Breisgau: Rombach, pp. 670–686.

Japan Visitor (date unknown), *Okamoto Taro*, http://www.japanvisitor.com/index.php?cID=416&pID=1435 Accessed 21 May 2013.

Jecu, M. (2010) 'Interview with Carlos Bunga', in F. Oliveira, *Carlos Bunga. The temporality of Space,* Lisbon: Athena**,** pp. 113–118.

Kant, I. (1998), 'Der Raum als Form der Anschauung (§ 2, Fs.–3)', in J. Timmermann (ed.), *Immanuel Kant, Kritik der Reinen Vernunft*, Hamburg: Felix Meiner Verlag, Koch, Neff & Oetinger & Co Publisher, A23/B38/98.4–15.

Kano, R., Batlle, M., Vautier, B. and the Ashiya Museum Japan (2001), 'Gutai', http://pagesperso-orange.fr/articide. com/gutai/fr/accueil. Accessed 21 May 2013.

Kaprow, A. (1966), *Assemblage, Environnements and Happenings*, New York: Harry N. Abrams.

Krogh Jensen, M. (2001), 'Mapping virtual materiality', in P. Weibel (ed.), *Olafur Eliasson: Surroundings Surrounded*, Massachusetts: The MIT Press, pp. 302–312.

Krome Gallery (2009), 'Marxitecture' (press release), http://krome-gallery.squarespace.com/exhibitions_bunga/. Accessed 29 May 2013.

Kubota, H. (2011), 'The Spinning Idol - Senjyu Kannon. Hironari Kubota Interview' in M. Jecu (ed.), *Subtle Construction*, Malmö, Lisbon: Bypass Editions.

Licata, C. (2007), Ei Arakawa and Amy Silman at the Japan Society, in *Art Criticism and Writing*, Fall Issue, http:// artcriticism.sva.edu/?post=ei-arakawa-and-amy-sillman-at-the-japan-society. Accessed 28 May 2013.

Mack, H. and Piene, O. (1973), (eds), *ZERO 1, 2, 3*, Massachusetts: MIT Press, p. XXIII.

Manovich, L. (2002), Generation Flash, http://www.manovich.net/TEXTS_07.HTM. Accessed April, 2014.

Massumi, B. (1998), 'Sensing the virtual, building the insensible', in S. Perrella (ed.), *Hypersurface Architecture, Architectural Design*, (Profile no. 133: 68, no. 5/6), May–June, pp. 16–24.

Matsuyama, N. (2007), 'Emergence of relationships: Interview with Yukihiro Taguchi', *Tokyo Art Beat*, http://www. tokyoartbeat.com/tablog/entries.en/2007/12/emergence-of-relationships.html. Accessed 28 May 2013.

Munroe, A. (1994), (ed.), *Japanese Art after 1945: Scream Against the Sky*, New York: H.N. Abrahams.

Nash, D. (date unknown), 'The story of Jack the Dripper', http://www.jackson-pollock.com/action-painting.html. Accessed 21 May 2013.

Newman, M. (1999), 'After conceptual art: Joe Scalan's nesting bookcases, duchamp, design and the impossibility of disappearing', in M. Newman and J. Bird (eds), *Rewriting Conceptual Art*, London: Reaction Books, pp. 206–221.

Okamoto, T. (1999), *Today's Art*, Tokyo: Kobunsha (unpublished and informal translations of the Japanese original, as the book has not yet been published in translation).

Olivares, R. (2008), 'The incomprehensible beauty of tragedy', editorial, *Exit Magazine,* (24), http://www.exitmedia. net/prueba/eng/articulo.php?id=190 . Accessed 28 May 2013.

Onbashira (date unknown), http://www.onbashira.jp/english/. Accessed 25 May 2013.

Osborne, P. (1999), 'Conceptual art and/as philosophy', in M. Newman and J. Bird (eds), *Rewriting Conceptual Art*, London: Reaction Books, pp. 47–66.

Ott, M. (2007), 'Virtualität in Philosophie und Filmtheorie von Gilles Deleuze', in P. Weibel, P. Gente (eds), *Deleuze und die Künste*, Frankfurt am Main: Suhrkamp, pp. 106–133.

Pacquement, A. (1987), 'Gutai; l'extraordinaire intuition et documents joints', in S. Takashina and G. Viatte (eds), *Japon des Avant-garde: 1910–1970. Repères Chronologiques et Documentaires*, Paris: Centre Georges Pompidou, pp. 280–288.

Papadakis, A., Cooke, C. and Benjamin A. (1989), (eds), *Deconstruction*, New York: Rizzoli International Publications.

Parr, A. (2005), *The Deleuze Dictionary*, Edinburgh: Edinburgh University Press, pp. 75–76.

Phelan, P. (2002), 'Building the life drive. Architecture as repetition', in P. Ursprung (ed.), *Herzog und De Meuron. Natural History*, Montreal: Lars Müller Publisher and the Canadian Centre for Architecture, pp. 290–299.

Plissard, M.-F., Derrida, J. and Peeters, B. (1985), *Droits de Regards*, Paris: Editions de Minuit.

Restany, P. (1982), *Yves Klein*, Paris: Hachette.

Ricoeur, P. (2006), 'Archives, documents, traces', in C. Merewether (ed.), *The Archive*, London: Whitechapel Gallery, The MIT Press, p. 67.

Philip Rousseau (2012), *A Companion to Late Antiquity*, West Sussex: Wiley Blackwell.

Silva, S. (2003), 'Interview with Pinksummer Galerie', *Pinksummer*, http://www.pinksummer.com/pink2/exb/sil/exb001en.htm. Accessed 28 May 2013.

Sao Paulo Biennal, http://www.bienal.org.br/FBSP/en/AHWS/Pages/default.aspx. Accessed 28 May 2013.

Sardo, D. (2007), 'Low-tech connections and performativity', in M. v. Hafe Perez (ed.), *Anamnese Catalogue*, Lisbon: Fundacao Ilidio Pinho, pp. 413–419.

Shimamoto, S. (date unknown), 'My avant-garde', http://www.sukothai.com/X.SA.16/X.16.Shimamoto.html. Accessed 21 May 2013.

------(date unknown), 'Official website', http://www.shozo.net/prof/indexe.html. Accessed 21 May 2013.

Takashina S., Viatte G. (1987), (eds), *Japon des Avant-garde: 1910–1970. Repères Chronologiques et Documentaires*, Paris: Centre Georges Pompidou.

Vidler, A. (2000), *Warped Space. Architecture and Anxiety in Modern Culture*, Massachusetts: MIT Press.

Vogl, J. (2007), 'Was ist ein Ereignis?', in P. Weibel, P. Gente (eds), *Deleuze und die Künste*, Frankfurt am Main: Suhrkamp, pp. 67–83.

Weibel, P., Gente, P. (2007), (eds), *Deleuze und die Künste*, Frankfurt am Main: Suhrkamp.

Wilson, L. K. (1996), 'Cyberwar, God and television: Interview with Paul Virilio', in T. Drucken (ed.), *Electronic Culture: Technology and Visual Representation*, New York: Aperture.

Wooley, B. (1993), *Virtual Worlds*, London: Penguin Books.

Yukihiro, T. (2008), 'The last chair', http://www.youtube.com/watch?v=oAtfegtI2vM. Accessed 23 May 2013.

Zero (1963), 'Manifest', http://de.wikipedia.org/wiki/Datei:ZERO-Manifest1.jpg. Accessed 21 May 2013. My translation into English from the German original.

Žižek, S. (1996), 'From virtual reality to the virtualization of reality', in T. Druckrey (ed.), *Electronic Culture: Technology and Visual Representation*, New York: Aperture, pp. 290–295.